PILGRIMS' GUIDE TO THE KINGDOM
Marion Morgan

Foreword
by Gerard W. Hughes SJ

First published by Shoreline Books November 1990
Revised Edition 2024. Searchline Publishing

© 2024 Marion Morgan

Illustration on this page by Michael Ivens SJ

Contents

	Page
Forewords	
1. Introduction	1
2. In the Beginning	2
3. Authority and Kingship	8
4. Holiness	14
5. Spiritualities	20
6. Conversion to Christ	30
7. Lord, Teach Us to Pray	37
8. Difficulties	46
9. Parish Life	54
10. Exile	65
11. Evil and Suffering	71
12. Hell	77
13. Abandonment	81
14. Winning the Battle: Resurrection	87

This book is dedicated to all who have helped me on my way.

Forewords to first edition

Pilgrims' Guide to the Kingdom is written by a lay woman, who is neither a professional theologian, nor a cleric, nor a member of a religious congregation, but she writes out of her own rich experience of lived faith. I hope her book will encourage other lay men and women to write and share their own insights.

The book consists of a series of Scripture-based talks given by the author, who is Secretary to the Greater Bristol Ecumenical Council. Her head and heart are in the Cloud of Unknowing, but her feet are firmly on the ground. It is this earthed quality of her thought which makes it such a valuable contribution to the most neglected ministry in the Church, the ministry of lay person to lay person.
Gerard W. Hughes SJ

Each chapter gives helpful and sharply focused application of the scriptures to contemporary Christian living. Our easy assumptions are challenged, whatever our spiritual tradition.
Rev David Gillett, Principal Trinity College, Bristol

From the author:

Pilgrims' Guide to the Kingdom was written and then first published in 1990 – a long time ago. Covid was unheard of. Global warming was not taken seriously enough. The Berlin Wall was still unassailed. There was no internet. But the truths I have tried to express remain the same and to try and update the historical aspects of the text would mean rewriting and rephrasing it completely. So please simply bear in mind that the world has changed since it was written, as has our understanding of it, but the writing is still valid in its own right and context.

1. Introduction

In my work with the Greater Bristol Ecumenical Council, in the seventies and eighties, I met many people of all denominations, all working very devotedly for various good causes; all contributing in their own ways to the total work and mission of the church, and the bringing of the Kingdom. Most would have had their own lives of prayer and worship.

Because of the demands of the work, it was very easy to lose sight of the overall perspective, the context within which this work was being done. This book was an attempt to spell out this context, in order to encourage pilgrims on the Way, and to help them to recognise features of the terrain through which they were travelling.

It is a guide, a sort of handbook. Like all general guides, it does not go into great detail on any one feature; rather, it outlines the main points of the landscape and indicates areas of interest which would repay a visit or merit further study. It mentions various hazards and pitfalls, with occasional hints as to how to circumvent or overcome them. It constitutes a sort of bird's-eye view of things.

Obviously, the subject matter has been treated in a slightly cavalier fashion, with many omissions. Some of the chapters started life as talks to groups or talks at services, usually ecumenical.

It follows roughly the framework of the Spiritual Exercises of St. Ignatius, which have been so formative in my own life.

I hope it will encourage all of us to become increasingly joyful as our pilgrimage progresses, and to recognise the marks of the Kingdom more and more in the ordinary events of our lives. I hope that it will help us all to 'keep on keeping on'. Most of all, I hope it will contribute to giving us a renewed sense of our own value, and of God's unimaginable love for us, a sense of destiny and of hope, so that we ourselves become truly a people of love and that that love infuses more and more the work that we are privileged to do.

2. In the Beginning

Let's start from the beginning — with the creation story in Genesis 1 to 3. To my mind, these chapters are some of the most beautiful and profound in the whole of the Bible. It is good to consider our origins from time to time; such pondering sets the context for all later meditations, and can bring reassurance and hope at the times when all seems dark and confused. Don't let the actual details or chronology of the story get in the way of the messages that the writers wanted to convey. It is these messages that are important and which I want to explore a little. They are rich and various, and at different levels. We shall keep coming back to them.

Creation is good
The central conviction is that creation is basically good. The text later goes on to explain how sin and toil entered the world, but does not alter its basic assertion: God created the world and all within it, and it was good. Indeed, it was very good.

In Job there is the assertion that at creation "the morning stars sang together and all the sons of God shouted for joy" (Job 38:7). The two notes of joy and of beauty permeate the first two chapters of Genesis.

All was created good, and this includes man and woman. They were to be the crown of creation; and stewards of it. They are intimately connected with it. They are created as part of it: a special part, but part of it for all that. We forget this intimate connection at our peril. We are not superior to it, nor apart from it: we are created and sustained by it. At death we return to it. We eat it; we drink it; we derive our health from it; we are affected by its moods and climates; by our own physical metabolism. In turn, our running of creation, our stewarding of its resources, directly affects it. We are only half living if we forget we are part of physical creation.

The 'pathetic fallacy' used by poets and dramatists, whereby nature is credited with human emotions, bears witness to our root belief in this.

So the first encouraging message is that all was created good, and that that includes us too. We need to believe this. Do we actually like ourselves? We may like our gifts and our talents, but what about just ourselves, apart from our gifts? We too were created lovable and good.

This means we must beware of false modesty, and be grateful for our gifts! They all come from God. Our intelligence comes from his intelligence; our beauty, from his beauty; our sense of humour, from his sense of humour. From where else could they come? We are made in his image and likeness! Our capacity for enjoyment comes from his capacity for enjoyment; our experience of being a parent, from his parenthood of us. Our compassion comes from his compassion. Our desire to do good also comes from him.

He did not just set the world off and then abandon it to its own devices. He holds it in being. It is his life pulsing through the universe and the world now, keeping it in being, according to his attributes. It is his energy and life that keeps us all in being. So, by looking at the world, and learning to understand it, we can learn more of God.

Immediately, we come up against the problem of evil. There is also ugliness in the world, and creation itself is "red in tooth and claw". How can we say that the good aspects are of God and not the bad aspects?

The text struggles with this problem and comes up with the inspiration that the option for wrongdoing was presented and that man chose wrongly; as a result of this, difficulties, pain, toil, drudgery entered the world.

Nature was created good, but rules and laws were built into its very nature to keep it so. If we abuse her, she does hit back. The balance is somehow maintained, ultimately, although we have a duty to preserve it. If we abuse our bodies we have warnings that this is happening and so are given the chance to correct the abuse. So also with nature. The pain in childbirth and the thorns and toil are seen as means of our correction and our opportunity for penance. We may wish to discuss the teaching, but it seems clear to me that that is how the writers of Genesis saw it.

This intimate connection of man with nature is seen again in the account of the crucifixion: nature itself turns on Jesus as he is scorched by the heat, tormented by flies, subject to the terrible pull of gravity on his hands and feet. But finally the sun is darkened, the earth quakes; creation itself groans in sympathy with this event, and bears witness to its cosmic and time-shattering significance.

It is possible to believe in a creation which could have been much less cruel than the one we have, had dark forces not played such a large part. The nature of these dark forces is a mystery where much exploration can still be done. Suffice to say that the writers of Genesis admit the presence of dark forces which alter the whole aspect of created reality.

Created with purpose
The reasons why God created the world are not stated, but the sense of purpose is plain. All was meant, and all was ordered. If we compare it with our own creative instincts, the act of creation brings joy in its very nature. Sometimes we create without any motivation apart from the joy of creating. We feel like making something. Human parenthood gives us insights into the joy of giving life to another being: the wonder, and the mystery of it. Perhaps God felt a bit like that about us, and about the world. The sheer abundance, generosity, proliferation, colour, variety and detail in the created world seem to bear witness to an intense pleasure in the creation of it.

Creation exists to show forth God's glory; to show what he is like, which is by nature glorious. Men and women can enhance nature, and can discover God within it. We can reveal him and his depths and wonders in art, science, music, engineering, and all our modern advances, as well as in more ancient arts like gardening and agriculture. We also were created with a purpose, and fulfilling that purpose brings meaning into our lives. Meaninglessness and boredom come from engaging in things cut off from God's will and purpose for us and for his world.

Creation is always relative. It is always less than the new Heaven and the new Earth which are promised for the future. It has limitations. But Jesus chose to enter into it, and we believe that in him it has a permanent value. What we do in this life is important, in the light of the next life. Even had there been no sin, Jesus might have come to show us how to live in and through creation and how eventually to transcend it and enter into another dimension of life.

Does this life contain its own meaning? I don't think so. I think we can only understand it in the light of the next life, after death.

Meantime, we are all stewards of creation. It is our job to run the world! But a steward cannot alter the basic principles on which the owner wants to run the estate. We have a brief, with guidelines. We run the world according to those guidelines. And we are accountable. God entrusted creation to us, but it is his. It can cry to him for vengeance. We will be asked to give account of our stewardship because ultimately it is in his control.

The increasing awareness today of ecological issues and our responsibility for the maintenance of the planet is entirely in keeping with these chapters, written so long ago.

But don't lose heart. Before man and woman had done anything, God blessed them, and he blesses us also. He wants us to succeed — he is on our side. He has given us a challenge. It is up to us to take it up — and he is waiting to help us.

Created in relationship
Throughout these first chapters of Genesis, there is apparent a very intimate and personal relationship between God and his first two created human beings. He walks peacefully with them in the cool of the evening, and talks with them.

Was there really an Adam and Eve? There surely was a first moment when two human beings found what it was to pray to a personal God. If we believe that God initiates prayer, and it is we who respond to this initiative, then there was a moment in history when God considered the time had come to begin to reveal himself.

We also know of those precious moments of intimacy with God — those moments when he draws very close to us.

We know as well of moments of joyous praise, when we pour out our hearts to him.

And we know of moments of adoration and awe — moments when we relate to God in the deepest recesses of our being. There are no words of praise at these levels of being — simply an utter attentiveness, or a silent outpouring, or a deep stillness. At such moments we are aware of the truth of things: that he is great and we really are his creatures.

Created in his image
We should take really seriously the fact that we are made in the image of God. Of course we are flawed: no one could be unaware of this. But the basic material of our complex being is good, and in the image of God.

The implications of this are infinite. It means that whatever we find in ourselves that is good tells us something of God. It means that whatever we find in ourselves or in this world that is bad presents a problem. It means that whatever we discover of God should find some answering chord in ourselves.

Everything that is good and which is appropriate to being human has its divine counterpart. Hence human happiness is a reflection of divine joy; human creativity reflects that of the divine; human authority reflects divine authority; human competence reflects divine omnipotence. Even human time reflects divine rhythm, divine cycle. We are promised a new Heaven and a new Earth. A life in heaven that consists solely of contemplative delights seems somehow to do violence to our human nature. What transformed human nature looks like we simply do not know. That it exists is witnessed by the resurrection and ascension of Jesus, and by our beliefs concerning Mary and all the saints.

Sin, suffering and toil, which form so much of our lives, are neither our beginning nor our end. Our beginning lies in a creation that was and is good; our end, through Christ, in a resurrection that is glorious. The darkness we find is the passage between light and Light; between life and Life.

In baptism, Christians believe that we begin our participation in the death and resurrection of Jesus. It marks the first step in our transition between ordinary human life and a life where we share in the divine nature of God, in Christ. The sacraments graft us on to the true vine, and we draw strength of a different order through them, through the company of other Christians, through the Word of God in Scripture, through the Holy Spirit. We become rooted in Christ, and more and more incorporated into him.

When we feel torn in pieces, or split in two, or at war with ourselves, this is simply the manifestation of a personality not yet fully grown, in a world not yet perfect. We are made in the Trinitarian image of God, and this is the source of our complexity. Our task, surely, is to learn to develop as many aspects as possible of our God-given variety within an integrated personality.

In the light of all this, what happened at the Fall? This capacity we have in ourselves for God, this gateway to the source of life and knowledge, was violated; raped even. The essential rule at this level of our being is that all is gift. Our attitude is one of passivity, even in activity. But by taking the fruit, man grabbed. Adam and Eve may or may not have been the first man and woman; they certainly represent the first man and woman to enter into a conscious relationship with God. But before the time was right, at the dictate of their own desire, they grabbed at the good things of God instead of waiting, in obedience, on the divine will. In so doing they violated their own deepest nature, and the disruption was of cosmic significance. Their disobedient wills were cut off from the peace and beauty of the will of God, their Creator. There was no way back; from then on, they and their descendants were to live in exile.

3. Authority and Kingship

One of the effects of being made in the image of God is that it feels quite normal to us to try and run the world. From our earliest age we try to control the circumstances around us and express anger and frustration when things go wrong. As we get older the range of our control can extend. Our path seems plain — and if only other people would just do this, or move there, our objects and goals would be obtained. It seems more and more unreasonable that other people do not adjust and adapt to our system. So we may try and force them to: by coercion, or persuasion, or manipulation; because our goal, our way, is right. Why can't they see it? Or, if they do see it, why can't they see that our method is right, not theirs? It is all so simple!

It seems to me that the world and our living in it consist of webs and patterns of amazing complexity: patterns consisting of relationships, cause and effect, contingent circumstances. And that these are part of a larger pattern again — that which we may call chance, or coincidence; pieces of a larger jigsaw intruding into our own.

At whatever point in the interweaving one is standing, it appears to be the centre: from this point, all radiates out, and all roads lead into it.

That is true of whatever point we are at, except the dead end.

This fact is powerfully illustrated by today's cities, or even by today's airports. Any one of them can be seen as the hub of the world's business. All are interconnected. Or take our road system: any one of the great interchanges can seem to be the centre of the system: all roads lead to it and all roads lead out of it.

How these multi-systems of people's lives are ever coordinated into a whole, only God knows. But it is quite plain that it is a moving, dynamic creation that we are dealing with. As circumstances and choices rearrange into different convolutions or formations, so directions of growth surely adapt to the new and continually changing situation. And beneath and through all is the concept of Providence. As Hamlet said: "There's a divinity that shapes our ends, / Rough-hew them how we will."

But often that Providence is further off than we like to think. It gives us wide scope for our own decisions and leaves us always, to a greater or lesser extent, responsible for them.

So, maturity begins when we realise that for every one of our plans there are other plans held by other people. Some of these may converge, which means the possibility of agreement, through discussion and negotiation. Some may clash, which means someone loses out on their ideas. But once we realise that there are different ways of looking at things, we move into a different way of living.

This initially can be confusing and frightening. We are no longer in control. It takes time to be able to live within different systems and not lose one's sense of identity, wholeness, base.

Business mergers often involve this. Church unity workers have to take it very seriously. It involves learning to live in one chosen situation whilst admitting the values of other situations. It means being content with seeing less than the full picture. It means trusting others to be conscientious in their parts of the whole, and leaving it to them to do — even though their actions and decisions affect my life. It means (a) limiting our areas of control, and (b) knowing that these very areas are provisional and relative. Whatever I do will be modified and altered by the person coming after me, and even by the people receiving my decisions, i.e. those who have to put them into effect. It may be that I do something of permanent value, but that is rare, and perhaps happens once or twice in a lifetime: and even then it may well be done before I have realised its significance.

Much more lasting is the authentic living out of who I am —few of us are called to be visible contributors to history. Our lived contribution to the world will somehow endure — and will certainly be part of eternity — but that which remains is not usually the actual decisions we make. It is more likely to be the spirit in which we make them.

In an increasingly plural world, the task of oversight, whether in business or in church affairs, becomes more and more complex and demanding. And, quite naturally, we tend to reduce the situation over which we preside to manageable proportions, the amount our brains can cope with. Anything beyond that confuses us and makes it impossible to operate, so we cut it out of our thinking.

The wider our vision, and the greater our capacity for detail, the more scope we allow for those within the orbit of our oversight. Hence, with God, there is the possibility for infinite variety. Each one of us can develop authentically and yet inter-relate and be part of God's overall purpose for the world. The more God is excluded from oversight, the more narrow and restricted it becomes. Hence the only way to be an effective boss is to allow one's own limitations to be constantly transcended; which feels like learning not to want your own way all the time.

The more able one is, the harder it is to learn to 'let go', to delegate, to allow others to participate (and sometimes get it wrong). To take an example close to home: we may know, for instance, that the flowers look better when we arrange them. But nevertheless is it possible that, when someone else does a chapel for us, badly, even then — if we look — we may see what they were trying to say through their arrangement, and learn something?

As a habit, of course, it is better that people who are more able should specialise, but in a church, is there not scope, on occasions, for breaking the normal rules of the world (where efficiency and success are the only real virtues) in order to learn something different?

How else are we to be released from our self-will, which prevents our growth into maturity? 'I do it my way!' Fine — yes. Have you ever tried, for fun, doing it someone else's way?

A minister leaving a parish said to his successor: "Mrs. X will do anything for you at the drop of a hat — her hat."

But how do we release our control over the world without descending into personal chaos? Only when we are sufficiently secure in love to do so. Only when we know and trust that those to whom we have committed our decisions care for us and will also try to do the best for us. When we have been hurt, badly hurt, by other people's decisions and actions, it is understandable that this is more and more difficult for us. Why are the young so against authority? Partly because they do not trust it, because it has let them down in a world with which it appears to be satisfied.

This self-will, which is self-defence, is widespread, almost universal. The way out is mutual trust, eased by love. It is the only way to freedom. Some people feel that the worth of freedom is such that they will accept the bad exercise of authority for the sake of it. Hence they will allow things to be done less well for the sake of not being dominated by their own desire to make all the decisions and to control everything. Where this involves the welfare of others, the dilemma is particularly acute.

If St. Teresa wished her nuns to plant onions upside down (which she didn't), the result would not be catastrophic, except for the onions. Were a religious or other superior with little or no knowledge of, say, teaching, to impose a plan which the teacher felt was damaging to the children involved, then there would be difficult questions of conscience and loyalty to be worked out.

The tension comes in working out these conflicts, at every level. The answer, surely, does not lie in denying the validity of authority. Where one admits the right of authority over conscience (i.e. the right of authority to direct and form a conscience), the problems can be even more acute; but the liberation of self can also be correspondingly greater.

Jesus' moral conscience might well have said to him that the scandal caused to the disciples and friends, the grief and pain to his mother, the teaching unspoken, the people unhealed, were sufficient cause to postpone the time of the crucifixion for at least a year or two, but his obedience to his Father was of deeper and greater import. That is no real analogy: our problem is that the 'father' who is our immediate superior (be he manager, or parish priest, or parish council) never quite seems to have the facts right! If we trusted him to have a fuller knowledge and greater understanding than ourselves, it would be far easier lovingly to obey him.

In the human condition, that knowledge and understanding can never be guaranteed. Hence our dilemma; and hence the reason and excuse, justified at so many levels, for the disobedience which has fractured and fragmented our world, our societies, our marriages, and even our churches.

Obedience worries me. It goes wrong so often. Childish obedience stultifies growth and is the cause of many scandalous and outrageous results. But even true childlike obedience does not always escape dire consequences. How does one balance a rightly responsible attitude, prophetic vision, passionate concern which must inevitably clash with established practices, with obedience? Only with heroic fortitude! Only by being "as wise as serpents and as innocent as doves" (Matt. 10:16).

If there is no one to whom you are obedient, it feels in effect that there is no one who cares for you. Obedience must always be two-way: allegiance in return for care. There cannot and should not be one without the other. Where both operate, the result can be liberating and beautiful, tender and teasing, gentle and strong. The commitment brings security, but should not mean the loss of adventure. The stronger the trunk, the further out the branches can reach.

To return to the original point: sharing in God's sovereignty is a right instinct and is good. It reflects man and woman's stewardship of the earth. We are in fact asked to run the world, to make decisions, to be responsible for the world and to be held responsible for it. We are accountable for our actions. Today, more and more people are becoming aware of this responsibility. With the technology and the communications systems that we have now developed, for the first time in history we may be able actually to fulfil our God-given task.

It is natural to created beings to be willing, to serve, to praise. Animals like to serve us: think, for example, of dogs and horses. However much we destroy nature, it keeps coming back for more: consider the weeds and flowers on building sites and demolished areas, or the persistence of grass. It is faithful to us, however much we abuse it. And we have all the means to abolish it utterly; have already destroyed irrevocably vast areas.

Christianity brought a new dimension to this existing order of being. When we participate in Christ's life, we also share in his kingship over all things. The stewards hand all back to the Father, in Christ, and he is then made king over all. We cannot imagine what this means. We know only that this, his kingship, will transcend all our intimations of it which we practise in this life, the reflection of his likeness and glory, here on earth.

4. Holiness

The more positive our view of creation, the more we are left wondering what it means to be Christian. If God as Creator loves everyone, what difference does it make to be Christian? If the service of one's neighbour is a value accepted and put into practice by many non-churchgoers, what more are we being asked to do?

Many Christians today have little idea of what they are aiming for in their Christian life, apart from being able to serve their neighbour more, and generally coping better with life. In fact, it does not seem quite right to us to think about aiming for anything! We may speak of 'closer union with God' or a 'closer walk with God'; of deeper prayer; of doing his will more perfectly; even of deepening our relationship with him; but on the whole our ideas are rather vague about what difference it will actually make to us. In this we differ from previous ages.

I do not think that the majority of Christians today aim for holiness. We might wish to be better people, or to serve the Lord better, or to love him more, but the goal of personal holiness is not one that one hears much about. Other ages did seem to aim for holiness, and a lot of the older type of spiritual writing takes this as a starting-point. Much of this writing comes from the monastic tradition, where the call to holiness was at its most explicit. Our age thinks far more about what it means to be human, fully human.

Without the goal of holiness, our faith can be undermined. If we become discouraged because our active efforts have suffered a setback, we have nothing to fall back on. If we see other people, non-churchgoers, doing better work than ourselves, our own Christian life can seem to be worthless. So a crux question for Christianity today is to do with what makes Christian wholeness different from human wholeness. Is Christianity just a repair operation, enabling us to be full and proper human beings (making it unnecessary if we can cope well without it); or is it something new, over and beyond what is available to unaided created humanity?

It is tempting to equate Christian holiness with full human integrity. We think of people who are mature, balanced, integrated, not self-centred — outgoing people without 'jerks' or hang-ups, who pray — and we see them as good Christians. We assume that a church is necessary to help them to become that sort of person. It is an attractive picture but, on closer inspection, it falls to pieces.

If we label as 'Christian' everything that is good, we are doing a disservice to God as Creator, worshipped by many religions, who created all things good. The world was good and goodness abounded before Jesus was born. The 'just man' was a recognisable person. Yes, there was sin as well, but efforts to contest and contain it did not begin with Jesus.

What do we mean by 'holy'? Do we just mean good? And is the possibility of holiness open to everyone, in spite of basic defects?

It is useful to remember the traditional distinction between objective and subjective holiness. Objective holiness is the full perfection of Christian being which I may hope to have in heaven. Subjective holiness is the most that is open to me here on earth, taking into account all my limitations of mind, body, and personality. With this as a starting-point, let us look at the sources of the idea of holiness. The most obvious one is the Bible.

In the Old Testament, holiness was linked with the glory of God: with the cloud over the tabernacle, and the other manifestations of his glory. It was also very definitely an attribute belonging to God. He imparted it to things or people. Vessels, places, etc. could be set apart and thus regarded as holy, but holiness itself stemmed from God and was given by him: "It is not by cult, ritual, observance or ceremonial that holiness is imparted; on the contrary, all holiness derives from the personal God who is himself holy." (Alan Richardson (ed.), A Theological Word Book of the Bible, SCM, 1957.)

Human beings are not holy by nature or by birth. They may be innocent, but not holy. A baby, for instance, may give every appearance of being innocent, but is not usually seen as holy.

Holiness, or sanctity, in the New Testament is used in two senses: it is both something given and something to be achieved, or completed.

In the Old Testament, the good man's response to the call to holiness was in worship, praise and behaviour. He tried to fulfil all the requirements of the Law; he aimed to be just in all his dealings, to be kind to the widowed and fatherless, not to oppress the poor, and so on. This looks very like the good, integrated twentieth-century person we were first considering. But throughout the Old Testament there are hints of something more: the time will come when God will pour out his Spirit on all flesh; the young men will see visions and the old men will dream dreams (Ezekiel et alia). In Ezekiel again: "I will give you a new heart ... and I will take out your heart of stone and give you a heart of flesh" (Ezek. 36:26).

They knew, as we know, that a person may do all the right things, but their heart may still be untouched. The virtuous people are not always the most loving people, and God wanted a people that is loving. Behaviour needs to spring from the heart to be acceptable in the Kingdom. Jesus came not to destroy the Law, but to fulfil it in ways deeper and more totally comprehensive than had ever been envisaged. And we are called to share in this.

The rich young man cried, "All this have I done since my youth! What more can I do?" It was a cry from the heart, because his heart was not touched by his good deeds. He went away sorrowful; but at least he had seen the problem. He had recognised the deeper level of self which also needed to be redeemed and brought into relationship with God.

Thought and action from the heart are at the same time both more demanding and liberating. To be Christian from the heart means we love from the heart, can find truth in the heart, can participate in glory from the heart. This is what Jesus means when he says that we are to be perfect. We are to aim for deeper and deeper conversion and dependence on him until at last the love from our deep heart wells up and flows through all our being and out to others, and out to him. That is the ideal for which we are striving.

This is not to say that everything should be done in an emotional manner. It is not to say that we feel loving all the time. We cannot. We are human. It would not even be appropriate. What we usually feel is only our version, our pale reflection, of the real thing; and when we feel nothing at all, it is often a stage towards feeling in a more real way. What often happens is that we start off doing something good at the impulse, yes, of a genuine feeling; the feeling goes away and we are left with the chores, and more chores — with more and more work: we can go very stale. Because the Christian ideal is so much deeper and greater, transcending mere humanity, it is only too easy to slip back into an old approach of simply doing the right things. This is not wrong. In fact, it is very good, as far as it goes. But when it comes to substituting 'doing the right thing' for the real Christianity of the heart, then there are serious problems.

Jesus, as far as we know, worked publicly and actively for only three years of the 33 years of his life. And we can assume he was intensely active in the summer months but probably less so in the winter. Even at his busiest, he spent nights in prayer. So, he had a long preparation; he had long periods in prayer; and he had times when — we assume — he was normally social, sharing meals with friends and chatting with people. In the light of this, we should not begrudge time spent preparing and helping ourselves to be more complete human beings. We should allow ourselves time for prayer and reflection, for social activities, and for just being ourselves, either with our families or just by ourselves. Otherwise, our lived Christianity will simply not be attractive to others. More seriously, we can spend all our time and energy on doing things, and in the end our Lord has lost us, our love and ourselves. And he counts that as a bad bargain.

But to return to holiness: it is not simply wholehearted dedication to a cause. The Sermon on the Mount gives clues to a radically different way of life. Values are turned upside down: the first shall be last, and the last, first. Those who mourn are blessed; the rich are the unhappy ones. Right behaviour is to be overtaken and subsumed into totally loving and generous behaviour; even sacrificial behaviour, when someone lays down his life for his friends.

The Kingdom of God is of the heart. Nothing else is good enough. But even all this does not necessarily bring holiness. There is a hint of something even greater: the new wine needs new wineskins. Unless a man is born again of water and the Spirit, he cannot enter the Kingdom of God. We must become new creatures. Holiness is given as we empty ourselves, or are emptied, of our old selves and are filled with the Spirit. Holiness is given as we are incorporated into Christ at our baptism and through the Eucharist and grow in the ongoing experience of his death and resurrection through the continual dying inherent in our fight against selfishness and self-centredness. Holiness is finally given when our old life literally dies and the new life within us goes on and receives its new form and body in heaven.

We are to become children of God, by his gift. The gift comes through the Spirit, and is possible because of the redemptive work of Christ.

The story of sanctity is the story of how people allowed themselves to be killed for God! Perhaps that is a negative way of looking at it. We could also say it is the story of how creative love, springing from deeper and deeper levels, gradually comes to permeate the whole of a personality and every level of its functioning, never destroying it. It is the story of how ordinary life-flows and energies are taken over by the Holy Spirit. This is not necessarily the Spirit in his dynamic forms; gentleness — quiet love — are as much gifts of the Spirit as the more dramatic ones which draw the publicity. The Spirit brings Christ to birth in us. The Trinity comes to dwell in us, in all its infinite variety: Father, Holy Spirit, Son; Son, human and Divine.

The perfection of holiness is thus the whole person transformed, although invariably we see holiness only in various stages of growth. Final holiness, including the holiness of the body, is for after death. With the incorporation of the Christian body into Christ, through baptism, and the Eucharist, when we eat his body and drink his blood; through the other sacraments and through the Word; in the Spirit: something radically new has entered into the human race and its history which has never been seen before, and is not seen in such complete form in any other religion. This is the uniqueness of Christianity. It is comprehensive and total in the depth of what it claims:

transformation of the whole person, body, mind and spirit; incorporation into Christ, and hence a sharing in the divine nature of God.

It is self-evidently not a quick process, nor one that happens overnight.

5. Spiritualities

How does this transformation happen? This is where all the variety comes in, and this is why it is so important not to try and limit God's work in a person to the pattern that we think is appropriate. There are as many ways of becoming transformed into him as there are people. But in spite of the individual path of each and every person, there are nevertheless broad streams of common experience: like different trees of the same species, and different species in the same genus — for example, a birch tree and an oak, both being trees. Different people will be roughly following the same way in different places at the same time. There are great sweeps of style across the centuries, even though the outward forms may change: for example, an active involvement in social problems will look very different this century from, say, six centuries ago in another place, but the challenges to the personality and to the inner Christian life of the person involved may be remarkably similar.

Often these different ways are clarified, exemplified, crystallised, in one great leader. Often they also have their 'degenerate form', their imitation form, as well as their genuinely human form and their specifically Christian form. Thus, quietism can be seen as the degenerate form of true contemplation. Contemplation can be the genuine appreciation of a sunset, or the same experience deepened with a recognised awareness of the presence of God. Busyness can be seen as the degenerate form of sacrificial service to others, which again has its explicitly Christian expressions.

It seems that today a concern for world justice is a mark of the life and prayer of many Christians. This reflects a concern for the world expressed by many who would not call themselves active Christians, and by many from other religions. The abuse of this awareness might be the ruthless exploitation of any part of the world now made possible by improved travel and communications — for instance, in some commercial transactions and in the worst forms of tourism.

In the nineteenth century there seems to have been a general interest in authority and power and 'big' figures: it was the era of great monarchical figures such as Queen Victoria, particularly in her role as Empress of India. In the Roman Catholic Church, it was the time when papal infallibility was defined, and when Ultramontanism (an over-preoccupation with hierarchy which became heretical) was rife.

There have been many moves and styles over the centuries: moves to the desert; moves into monasteries; movements in popular piety; movements in the active apostolate; different movements in missionary activity; movements towards contemplative piety; movements towards social reform; in our own time, the renewal or 'charismatic' movement. Another major feature of our time is the number of different styles actually current; and, together with this, the movement towards unity among the major denominations, attempting to heal divisions that have lasted centuries. Even the vision and desire for unity is something rediscovered in a new way in recent decades. There have been many great names in Christian history, and it is pointless to quote at length. Just examples: Antony and Benedict; Julian, Rolle, a Kempis and Eckhart; Francis; Dominic; Teresa and John of the Cross; Ignatius; Wesley; Reformers and their followers; martyrs of all denominations.

Canonised Christian saints are slightly different. Catholics believe they are raised up by God to fulfil a particular purpose; to demonstrate a particular way of being Christian; to restate a particular Christian truth. Many of them have founded or reformed religious orders (for example, Benedict, Francis, Teresa). They are not necessarily the best — i.e. the most good — people around! They are called to be what they are for the sake of other Christians: a gift to us to help us to understand, to inspire us, to help us by showing how it can be done. Canonisation is primarily the formal recognition by the Church that their way of following and serving Christ can be followed or copied safely — that they were not deviants. They are given to the Church: the extra graces and help they were given were not primarily for their own good. This accounts for the sort of 'forced growth' quality to be found in so many of them, especially those who died young. They reach earlier than most the point of maturity and perfection of love that we all hope to attain eventually, more usually at death or afterwards. They are an extension of the help and advice we receive from good and holy people that we know in ordinary life. And we can meet most of them fairly directly through their writings and/or biographies.

If you do follow someone, it should lead to greater freedom, not a loss of individuality. It is an example of the group dimension, the making communal of a private prayer style. You meet others of like mind and spirit and draw help from (and give help to) them. As, for example, we are English with national characteristics, twenty-first century people with, again, appropriate characteristics, but we are also drawn usually into one of the great streams, or families, of spiritual tradition. These can often, though not always, cross denominational boundaries.

One of the criteria of a new tradition is that it should awaken recognition and response among others: 'Of course!' is the sort of reaction to be expected. Some people (for example, John Henry Newman) are way ahead of their time, but sooner or later what they say or how they live finds answering chords. Mavericks are to be regarded with suspicion!

Any discussion of a particular spirituality must take very seriously the fact that we are human; it is a way of becoming Christian in the particular human circumstances and language of our time and our place. Hence all traditional spiritualities have to be, from time to time, re-interpreted, re-found and re-translated into a new historical setting, because they were all historical to start with. If they do replant, that is one test of their vigour, authenticity, and eternal value and significance. All must be rooted in Scripture and in Christ to be Christian spiritualities.

Some specialise in Christ's teaching ministry, some his healing, some his penitential and redemptive work, some his priesthood, some his apostolic preaching, some his hidden years, and so on. Because baptism brings us into his life and death and resurrection, the new life is very directly linked to the actual life of Jesus, even though it finds quite new expressions, and even though many human experiences (such as old age) were not lived by Jesus. That is one thing that differentiates Christian new life from ordinary human good life: it is deliberately and consciously linked with Christ. And its holiness recognises the Other, the transcendent, and names it as Trinity.

Lay spirituality
Many books on spirituality and spiritual growth in past centuries have been written from the monastic context and been addressed mainly to members of religious orders or priests. Recent years have seen a greater emphasis on lay spirituality. It is worth spending some time considering the resources available today to lay people who wish to develop and strengthen their inner Christian life, and to note any particular marks which could distinguish such a lay spirituality.

The word 'lay' in English is always a little confusing as it can mean two things: amateur, as in lay psychology or lay electrician; or in strict ecclesial terms, those who are not ordained. In the latter sense, there is no implication that all non-clergy are non-professional in their prayer! So when we explore the term 'lay spirituality', the borders can become very blurred. What is usually meant is the spirituality appropriate to those who are neither clerical nor members of a religious order; but the term then covers everyone from those who spend all their time in working specifically for the church, through those who have full-time jobs elsewhere but are trying to deepen their prayer life, to those who merely attend services at Christmas and Easter.

The parish is the immediate and obvious focus for the spiritual nourishment of the laity. It can be a source of inspiration and life, or, in some sad cases, a major hindrance. One of the marks of lay spirituality is that you are very much a victim of liturgical circumstance. You may have no say at all as to the times of Masses or other services. In many areas and traditions it is simply not possible to attend a daily or even a weekly Eucharist. The style of celebration or service can vary enormously between one church and another and you either accept what is offered or go elsewhere. The latter option is one taken by many, though not open to all. Being prepared to travel and so being able to choose a church where one feels at home and able to worship and join in, can help considerably, but it does of course raise problems for those left behind.

One advantage of church unity could be a greater variety of worship available in any one geographical area, without difficult changes of allegiance.

As a lay person, the structure in which one's Christian life is expressed publicly is minimal — for example, attendance at church once a Sunday. Anything extra (or even this commitment) is subject to deliberate choice. Many people who find this insufficient align themselves with wider structures, many with their own rule of life: for example, the Third Orders (Franciscan, Carmelite, Dominican, etc.); or communities such as the Coventry Cathedral Community of the Cross of Nails. A parish sometimes adopts a minimum rule of life for those who are seeking closer bonds. In the Roman Catholic Church, the Society of St. Vincent de Paul is in a similar tradition. Although the emphasis is very much on charitable works, it is based in prayer and a recognisable spirituality. In the Church of England there are organisations such as the Guild of Health or the Julian prayer groups which also provide ways of deepening prayer life on a wider basis than simply the parish. These are usually open to all denominations.

Many lay people (not just Roman Catholics) are now reading the Divine Office regularly.

The retreat movement is growing in all sorts of forms among all traditions. The eight-day Ignatian retreat is popular; there is a demand, albeit smaller, for the 30-day Ignatian retreat; weekends of prayer are always well-booked, and there is an increasing number of days of recollection, quiet days, weekends, etc. among all denominations. Those who go away to such retreats sometimes form a link with a particular retreat house or conference centre, and will visit regularly for a short time of quiet and perhaps some spiritual direction. There are also various forms of group and individual retreats given in private homes.

Pilgrimages are becoming more and more popular.

A far greater number of lay people are involved in house groups, prayer groups etc. These take many forms and are usually ecumenical. Some groups study a specific topic — a book during

Lent, or a particular study booklet on a topic such as racial justice. Some concentrate mainly on Bible study; others are mainly silent (engaging in contemplative prayer); others again are in the 'charismatic' tradition (or Renewal Movement). Some focus specifically on intercession. All will involve joint prayer and the sharing of insights and experience. Such groups are often the most vital part of a person's growing prayer life.

It seems to me that, in the Free Churches, Fellowship meetings are in this tradition, although they involve a bigger group of people. Such meetings may consist of a hymn, prayer, a talk, notices and perhaps a cup of tea. People draw a lot of sustenance from them. The Mothers' Union, and the Union of Catholic Mothers, also have a spiritual content, providing a means of mutual support and encouraging growth in understanding of the living of the Christian life. Parish training programmes can also be a source of deep nourishment.

Another way of feeding lay spirituality is through books and other ways now available such as podcasts, radio and television. There is an enormous amount written on prayer at present, together with the re-issue of many of the classical writings and autobiographies. There are quite a few religious programmes, on both television and radio, and a proper assessment of these would be of great interest to many. Often the main contact with 'religion' that the non-church going public has is the Songs of Praise programme or its equivalent on other channels. We are a hymn-singing nation and have a rich and still growing heritage of hymns. It can be the starting-point for conversation with a non-believer.

Another interest of both believer and non-believer alike is the search for understanding of what it is to be human. Courses on personal growth or self-understanding or on relationships are always popular, as are books and programmes on psychology, counselling, etc. There is a genuine and deep interest in knowing who we are and how we function. Although not specifically religious (any more than physical medicine and health care are specifically religious), it can remove obstacles to growth and happiness and prepare a person for a fuller religious life — even help him/her to see the need for it. It has also led to a greater appreciation of the need to listen to people (and to be listened to) and the realisation that this is a ministry in its own right, and one very appropriate to a church.

There is a danger that some of these newer forms of growth and nourishment will seem available only to the educated and reasonably well-off. With the disappearance of some of the old forms of popular devotion and no real replacements this is something to be watched. But there are still some processions of witness and many public processions of support for good causes. As has been mentioned, there is an increase in interest in going on pilgrimage: a very ancient means of deepening devotion.

Lay spirituality encompasses the two main thrusts of all spirituality: outwards, towards an appreciation of the goodness of creation, seeing the need for redemption, and working actively in the Spirit for the liberation of all things and the bringing of the world to its fulfilment, in Christ; and inwards, towards the depths of the unknown God within ourselves. These two aspects of the same heartbeat, outwards and inwards, growth and renunciation, have to be kept in balance. So, going to work is working for the realisation of God's purposes in creation, and revealing more of who he is. Exploring one's personality or improving one's physical health is fitting oneself to make the best possible contribution one can towards the new Heaven and new Earth which are promised. Sharing in a group is recognising the corporate and social dimensions of our being. Working for justice is an essential part of our responsibility as stewards of creation.

But the other side is equally as important. We need to allow time for solitude and withdrawal. We need to be able to understand the suffering of the world and its part in redemption, and to learn how to bear it. With the many different pressures of church life, work life, family life, social life, travel, responsibilities, the lay person can find the means of integrating his world only deep within his own being. Karl Rahner prayed to the Father to make a unity out of the plurality of his busy life, and this is a prayer peculiarly appropriate to lay life; perhaps to religious and clerical life too. We all need to withdraw and sink down into the depths of ourselves in order to discover a perspective where the fragmentation of our lives is seen to be peripheral and the unifying force, or Spirit, is seen to be central to our being.

Perhaps in earlier monastic days, the exterior structure of the life safeguarded against fragmentation. Today, the lay person who wants to pray has no such structure, but the very pressures of life can launch him/her into an intense prayer. They can also drive a person to seek solitude. How else can we account for the increase in weekend and holiday cottages? Why else do people seek the anonymity and silence of a city centre church just for a few moments' respite? We need to pray and contemplate in order to survive.

So, recognising the current important move towards small groups, base communities, a deeper appreciation of being corporate, it is well to recognise also the equally important need to safeguard opportunities to be silent and alone, so that at a deeper level we may find God and thus infuse peace and unity into a distracted and divided world ... the world in which lay people are privileged to live and work and pray.

'Light-on' and 'light-off'
One important point that does need to be made is one that Ruth Burrows makes so clearly in her book Guidelines to Mystical Prayer (Sheed & Ward, 1976). She describes two people who have both achieved a very considerable measure of 'death to self' and rebirth in Christ — the sort of deep, serene, Christian integration you sometimes see in devout old people, old ministers, priests or nuns, missionaries. These two were in fact both Carmelite nuns. But one reached this stage through experiences of which she was very much aware — recognisable, diagnosably 'religious' experiences in the accepted sense of the word. The other was only aware of struggling in darkness, in the ordinary, rarely enlightened, humdrum circumstances of everyday life. Yet somehow, through constant giving in various ways, she was aware that some deep union had been given her; the 'divided self', and the struggles, though still around, had lost their power. Ruth Burrows refers to these two different modes as 'light-on' and 'light-off'. They are equally valid. Each must be tolerant of the other. But, in particular, no one should feel second-rate if they do not have religious experiences in the 'light-on' sense.

Another great divide is between the active and the contemplative ways. Value judgments here are not helpful! It may be that the contemplative way is seen as the 'better part', but that does not necessarily mean that I should be following it. Nor, surely, does it mean that the active way is second-rate. The only criterion for subjective holiness is the extent to which I personally am responding to Christ's call to me, now. This can certainly be a call to contemplative prayer, whatever my situation, but it may also be a call to greater involvement in the active struggle for justice in all aspects of my personal, social and ecclesial life; or simply involve a greater freedom and willingness in doing what circumstance dictates.

Growth in holiness does not equate with growth in sensible awareness of God. And we can never judge our own holiness or even force its growth. We can put obstacles in the way, or fail to respond, but basically it is all God's gift and God's invitation. It is something we may ask for, in prayer, and in his grace, but we have to be willing to accept the consequences of our prayer — and that in itself requires yet more grace. Our part is to respond to his promptings wherever and whenever we can, and to bear the pain and the joy that this brings.

This means also being content with the particular degree of holiness to which at this moment he is calling me, and being content with my limitations and my knowledge that others appear to be better. But who knows? We are never competent to judge anyone; God only knows the struggle a person has had to make to become the person they now are. Surely we are judged by our struggles, not by our results, particularly when the 'givens' of personality and circumstance vary so dramatically between one person and another. And to accept my limitations does not mean that I do not continue to struggle to transcend them.

Acceptance and respect for different traditions and different ways of being Christian are, I think, one of the most important aspects of today's spirituality. In previous ages (for instance, from the sixth century to the twelfth), the picture was very much more monochrome. Nevertheless, future ages will look back at our age and pick out our strengths and our weaknesses with greater ease than is possible to us. Our job is to respond authentically now, so that future ages may read the pattern we have made.

6. Conversion to Christ

The evangelistic rally is now an established part of English church life, especially in the major cities. With this in mind, it may be helpful to explore a little what we mean by 'conversion to Christ', and how such an experience relates to other experiences of church life.

The first creed of the early Christians was "Jesus Christ is Lord". The test of whether or not you were a Christian was whether you could say that, meaning that you recognised that he was God, and you gave him your allegiance. After that you were baptised.

Most Christians in England today are baptised as babies and are brought to church by their families long before they are at an age to make any decision about it. Even after they make their baptismal vows their own at confirmation, they may never have been brought to the point of consciously saying "Jesus Christ is Lord". This does not mean that their baptism is not 'working': on the contrary, there may be a real growth in faith. Nevertheless, if such a person were moved to respond to an appeal at an evangelistic rally, they might rightly feel that the issue had never been put to them like that before; they had not realised what the Christian invitation really was; they had 'missed out' on it, and the church was at fault.

It is important that we begin to understand what may be happening in such a person. An analogy can be made with marriage. To those of us who have been brought up in the church, becoming consciously Christian in a meaningful way can be rather like marrying the boy next door. Early childhood prayers can lead to a sense of friendship with the Lord. This friendship can be developed: in older childhood and adolescence, he can be asked to help in the choice of career, relationships, difficulties, and so on.

Now just as in ordinary friendship we can sometimes suddenly see someone we have taken completely for granted with 'new eyes'; just as a person can fall in love with someone they have known for years; so we can sometimes go through a stage where we are captivated by the Lord. We can be taken over by it all, and can bubble over with it. We express this joy in hymns and songs and in our behaviour. The enthusiasm of a new convert who wants to go around telling everyone about it has a lot of similarity with someone who has just got engaged. This stage also brings commitment: we decide to love and serve him in a new way.

This stage of commitment is signified in sacramental church life by confirmation, or adult baptism, or even renewal of baptismal vows. It surely cannot matter that it does not coincide with it. It is important that there is a sacrament to mark this point. It is important that there is an inner experience, a response in faith, that relates to the sacrament. Perhaps the fact that these two do not always coincide is part of our imperfect human condition; it is also due to the fact that we must be structured socially and each individual's special timing cannot always be met. What is important, surely, is that both aspects are recognised and developed.

The analogy of the Christian life with marriage can be taken further. The formal commitment in an ecclesial context can be likened to the actual wedding ceremony in marriage. Most people would agree that, although the wedding ceremony is meaningful and important, the hard work usually begins shortly afterwards! A wedding ceremony without a marriage of lives would be nonsense. Marriage surely means growing more and more into a unity with one another, a creative unity. Where a marriage is successful, the loving union reached at the end of life can be very inspiring. The Christian life is about union with Christ: a union that permeates all areas of our living and all areas of our being and personality.

Some people never seem to experience the 'falling in love' stage. Arranged marriages can nevertheless issue in real, loving, uniting marriages. Other people may remain sweethearts all their life long: this is often a matter of temperament. Surely value judgments should not be made one way or the other.

The timing of the wedding also varies. An early marriage, in the 'teens, leaves a lot of growing together and mutual learning about each other to be done later; but a real commitment to each other can be made. This commitment can be renewed as the partners mature, and can take place at deeper and deeper levels of their personalities.

A marriage of two mature people is of a different nature, and requires adjustments at different levels. Love at depth may flow sooner in time than with the young couple, because they may have already learned what loving involves.

Another analogy that can be made is the scriptural one with bread. Seed is sown, grows, is reaped, beaten, sifted, bruised, ground, made into flour, then dough, left to rise, then baked, and finally given to be eaten. 'Conversion' is usually seen to be at the reaping stage.

But it is misleading to think that in any one person Christian life goes smoothly from one stage to another. Sometimes it feels more like being on a spiral staircase where we are brought back to the same point time and again, each time with a new perspective. We need to look again at what we mean by conversion.

Perhaps we all have some idea of the end result of a Christian life: a glowing, dynamic, kind, radiant, serene, loving person in whom Christ really lives. Christ in him/her loves, compassionates, serves, teaches, suffers, laughs. The saint is a 'new person in Christ', body, mind, soul and heart; a full being, totally given to Christ. This given-ness, this giving of ourselves in response to Christ's invitation, is the core of what we mean by conversion. True giving requires freedom of will, an act of will. I freely, willingly, give an aspect of myself to Christ in response to his love. This aspect of myself may be a part of my will, my intellect, my memory, my mind or my understanding, my heart or my body. There is no right order for these decisions and gifts: the way each person is led by the Spirit along these paths is individual. Some decisions are more obvious than others: together, they mean growth, conversion. The sum of all these decisions is at our death when we say or enact: "Father, into your hands I commend my spirit" (Luke 23:46).

Hence the decision of someone who comes forward at a rally is one decision, a big one perhaps, but only one among many that have been made and will have to be made throughout a Christian life.

There are other decisions which seem to prepare the way for these 'converting' decisions. Many are to do with learning a certain detachment from things or values which we take for granted.

Our assumptions may be challenged through domestic crises — for example, a redundancy, an illness, a bereavement, or even a particular conversation with someone. Something gets through to us and makes us stop and think. Here is an important decision: we either carry on exposing ourselves to the situation or person that presented this challenge to our thinking and caused us to 'stop', or we close our minds and carry on as before. This may be the most crucial and fundamental decision: whether or not to close the door to growth and challenge.

Becoming involved in caring work often makes us rethink whole areas of our life. We have to decide to remain willing to help, to love people, with all its terrible implications.

As people come to find a deeper level of being, they may begin to ask about meaning: What is life all about? And they have another fundamental choice: whether to believe there is a meaning and to keep seeking it, or to give up the search. Perhaps the saddest people are those who have stopped searching.

All these choices can be seen as preparatory to consciously Christian decisions. They come to all human beings. The point at which any of these decisions leads to an explicitly Christian decision (if ever) varies with each individual. The story of the Last Judgment in Matthew, from 24:31 onwards, is worth considering: "Truly I say to you, as you did it to one of the least of these my brethren, you did it for me." The challenge of responding to Jesus, in all his ways of coming, is immediate for all humanity.

Within the church, there are more specific ways of preparing for, or making, converting decisions — i.e. decisions which lead to deeper dependence on and a deeper commitment to the Lord.

Different forms of penance or asceticism, different devotions, even different forms of active service, should all bring us to points where we open ourselves up, by our choice, in the Spirit, to the grace of God in Word, sacraments and prayer, and so allow ourselves to grow. At the very least, we have all known points where we could have turned away, and did not.

Decisions made at evangelistic rallies are specific and conscious decisions to follow Jesus. They may need to be interpreted. Those concerned may need to be shown that the past has helped them to this point, and that their present experience is the beginning of the future. They are at just one stage in a long process.

For all of us, it is helpful to list the religiously significant moments in our life, so we can gain some idea of the continuing action of the Spirit in our lives. We need to speak of our past experience of the church and of prayer; of choices that we have seen as significant and of how we have responded. Then, for those who have just been 'converted', it is possible to see more clearly what choice has actually been made, and at what depth. For all of us, it can lead to a greater appreciation of where we are, and of the direction in which we are now being called.

The call to be Christian is ultimately a call to sanctity, to holiness; a call to embark on a long and arduous journey, infinitely worthwhile. To be Christian is to be called to be a saint.

Conversion does also involve a turning away from sin; a turning from old habits which have not been helpful to us, to other people, or to God. For the new convert, this may be a fairly obvious exercise at the beginning. One of the difficulties of trying to deepen an existing conversion and commitment is that often we have very little real sense of sin. We are aware of doing our best and of trying to carry on, often in the middle of great difficulties, and it is very tempting to leave the rest to God. This may well be better than being too preoccupied with things that may be wrong. But the Christian life is meant to be joyful, and one of the main effects of sin is that it destroys our joy. We feel jaded and old and inflexible; drawn, even cynical. Our spontaneous enjoyment of life has gone.

This is not the place for an analysis of sin, or a detailing of ways in which we do sin. Perhaps it is more helpful to take the fact of sinning for granted, and see what can be done about it.

The first step is to name the sin; to face up bravely to the facts. The next step is to repent; to try to turn away from it and resolve to have nothing more to do with it. The third step is to say 'sorry' from the depths of our heart. The fourth step is to know ourselves forgiven. Receiving absolution, either in a sacramental context, or in some other way, is part of most Christian traditions. Some way of making amends is also part of many traditions.

How do we see our sin when sin brings its own blindness? Once we have done wrong, the very fact of doing it somehow justifies it to ourselves. We need something from outside to bring it home to us that this was unworthy, or to stir our conscience.

How do we repent when we really have not done much wrong and we know the pressure we were under? We really do not think it matters very much.

How can we say 'sorry' and mean it — say it with real compunction? What difference does it make, whether we are forgiven or not? Is not God somehow partly to blame for making the world like this anyway?

These are real questions and, if we find ourselves asking them, must be taken seriously. They must be brought into our prayer. Only God can show us the answers. Only in the Holy Spirit can we be melted and shown the reality of things. The real and genuine 'fear of the Lord' is a gift of the Holy Spirit. Only the gift of true repentance can free us from crippling and debilitating guilt complexes.

When we say that Jesus saves us from our sins, we are not just talking of abstract facts. He redeems and heals the effects of our sinfulness in ourselves, and the effects of the sin done to us by others. As this work grows in us, our love and gratitude also grow, in a way that feels natural, because we feel so much better. Our quality of life improves. We can enjoy more, relax more.

From the most selfish point of view, it is worth doing something about our sins!

All such work on ourselves is a work of the Spirit. It is supernatural, requiring more than our unaided abilities, by definition. It does not exclude professional help, by priests, ministers, therapists; or help from friends. We all need help in coming to terms with damage done to our personalities by events in the past. It involves bringing the damage to the Lord for healing; showing him our pain and asking for help. This help comes in many ways.

So, in this prayer to be shown our sins, we are not looking for frenzied 'nit-picking', nor intense introspection and self-analysis to induce a sense of sin. Rather, we rest in trust and in peace in the kind and gentle hands of the Lord, waiting in confidence for him to show us our failings. We sit at his feet, and allow him to see us; allow him to see us in all the different situations of our life. We let him into the corners of our mind and of our memories, where perhaps no one has ever set foot before.

We wait in confidence because he does answer this prayer of ours for enlightenment, because it is his greatest wish to help us and heal us, and to free us from all that harms us. For this reason he came to earth.

7. Lord, Teach Us to Pray

Prayer is important. I expect most Christians would say that prayer was the most important thing about the Christian life. It is largely what makes it Christian, as distinct from worthily human. Living in the image of God our Father who created us is open to all people, not just the Christians, and we are all made to be the crown of creation; we have been appointed stewards of creation. Helping our neighbour also is part and parcel of being human, not solely of being Christian. We all know really good, serving people, who do not admit to being in any way religious. All creation is made in the image of God. He is the Father of all who live. But prayer invites us to enter into a relationship with this, our Father. He invites us to get to know him. And Christian prayer invites us to pray to the Father in Christ; to get to know his Son and to receive the Spirit; eventually, to become incorporated into him.

Any growth in prayer is a growth in this relationship: a deepening of our understanding of his ways; a deepening of our dependence on him; a deepening of our giving of ourselves to him. It also means a growing knowledge of ourselves. The more we discover of ourselves — our enormous potential, our gifts, our 'lovableness', as well as the ways in which we are flawed and have been spoiled — the more we can invite him to share in all this, and the more he reveals himself to us as the God of great mercy and love, of beauty and joy.

Sometimes we think of God as the one who meets all our needs: who heals us, forgives us, answers our prayers. It is as if he can have no existence unless we give him something to do! Real prayer is a discovery of who God is, regardless of us; what he is like; how he is. Then we respond in adoration, or by entering into a real relationship with him, as distinct from forever asking him to join himself to us. But in every relationship there is a two-way flow of love: us to the Other; the Other to us. If it gets a bit one-sided, a bit 'me-orientated', that is part of our human condition. It is something else we can bring to him in prayer for healing. The petition, "Hallowed be thy name", puts prayer in a right perspective. It doesn't actually begin and end with us. We should at times focus entirely on the Other.

There is so much to be said about this relationship. Like all relationships, it needs to be worked at. Things will get in the way, which need to be talked out and healed. Sometimes these are things that we feel we are being asked to do and cannot face. The absolute key is to be honest; not to be afraid of what we really feel. He is big enough to cope! Only if we honestly start from where we are can he respond and lead us through into the deeper and deeper levels of love and joy and mystery which he wants to share with us. We will bump into the cross; there is no avoiding it. But we don't have to face it alone. We must share this with him, and with great courage try to tease out the pain, and carry on — otherwise we will simply come to a full stop. No one suggests it is easy, but there are great rewards in sticking with it.

St. Ignatius of Loyola has a wonderful prayer where he enters into a mutual sharing and exchange of gifts, as between lovers. Our Lord wishes to share with us all the gifts and graces of his resurrection life; all the joys of heaven; all the wonders and intricacies of his beautiful personality. In return, we give to him our talents, our gifts, our love, in an act of deep love and offering.

But it doesn't always feel like that. In fact, very often prayer doesn't feel like anything at all. I would like to spend a few minutes on the practicalities of prayer. I find the main difficulties lie not in praying, but in preparing to pray! Mind, we all know of the times when we have actually cleared a space in our lives, settled down to pray, and nothing happens. But there are also the times when we have made a special effort to come to a service, say, when it was really difficult and there were other things which were really pressing to be done, but in the end we forced ourselves and came — and it turned out to be a time of great blessing, and helpfulness. If we live in a family (and most of us do), there is so much noise: television, demands, the internet, mobile phones. It really is very difficult actually to make a quiet space in order to pray. Now I know that we can pray when we are doing the washing-up, driving the car, or pursuing any other activity. Those are the very lifelines of prayer — even the life support machines! But it is also most important to set aside a time which is only for prayer, even if it is only 15 minutes. But if it is only going to be for 15 minutes, it may be necessary to prepare for it first — for example, by playing music for a time before you really begin, just to quieten down and let the pressing odd thoughts come to the surface before you start. I always have a pen and paper handy: then I jot those odd thoughts down so they don't distract me any more ("Rosemary's birthday — Monday!" or " Put the recycling out"). Spiritual books can be a real help towards concentrating the mind. Recommended books are sometimes good — or just browse and see what takes your fancy. That can lead to quite surprising steps forward. Don't despise novels as a means to prayer! We lead such busy lives that an hour with a good novel with your feet up often allows all sorts of emotions to surface and be expressed. This loosens everything up, and so makes prayer easier when you turn yourself to it. But I find that a good novel which I know well and am re-reading slowly quite often leads me into direct prayer.

Actually going into a church can sometimes be the only way of ensuring a few minutes of undisturbed prayer — just sitting or kneeling before the Lord and seeing what comes. Again, it need not be for long: fifteen minutes is quite a good length. Five minutes is a bit short: I find I am just beginning to calm down when it is time to go. Thirty minutes on a busy day can become a bit of a worry because of the pressure of other things, or it can become a worry just because you can feel slightly cut off from the world and other people. Fifteen minutes can be just right. Even to do this once a week somehow gives more strength to the other ways of prayer that I use during the ordinary days.

If you live alone, it often feels as if it should be easier to pray. It probably is — but it may also be that when we turn off the television to pray, we become swamped with our own loneliness, or we lose ourselves in a hundred jobs. But it is worth persevering — bringing these very problems to the Lord for his help and healing. And there are so many good books these days which help with prayer, and with ways of quieting the mind. The person who lives alone has very special opportunities, of great value to the church as a whole.

Sheer fatigue and lack of concentration often frustrate our efforts, but the tiredness can lead to a different kind of prayer. It can sometimes be a help if we can really reach the centre of ourselves and pray from there, with the chattering, everyday self temporarily silenced. And if we are exhausted from doing good works, then the Lord often comes very close to us.

There are so many ways of praying — group prayer, liturgical prayer, different techniques for meditation, praying from Scripture, and so on. Prayer is a relationship. We can relate from every aspect of our personality — hence so many ways of praying. We can pray physically — lighting candles, for instance. Posture is important: kneeling, sitting, lying prostrate, standing at a window or by a doorpost. Experiment around — find the way in which you are being invited now. You may even pray in different ways at different times of the day or week. Encourage this! (I am a great believer in the weekly cycle for prayer — develop a routine whereby you include your prayer-quota for the week. Days are so unpredictable!)

Because there is so much variety around today, it is very important not to feel threatened by anyone else's ways. St. Anselm said: Pray as you can, not as you can't. What I have said may not relate to you at all. You may have your own way which I haven't mentioned, and you may find it helpful and not want to try altering it at the moment. Fine. I'm simply making suggestions that may help. We should always feel free to reject what does not feel helpful to us. We follow our instincts in our relationships with other people; so we should also in prayer. We should develop confidence in our own way so that we can wish people well in their ways! In God's grace, we usually find a few others who are of our 'genre'. Watch for this — see where you are drawn.

In all prayer, we believe that it is God, in the Spirit, who takes the initiative. He draws us; in his grace, we respond. We can only follow the promptings of the Spirit, and pray for the grace to do so. God deals with each one of us individually. Yes, we relate also in groups, but God has a very special respect for the individual. He knows the right pace for us. Sometimes it seems slow; at other times it seems a bit too fast. The important thing is not to watch other people and compare ourselves. As Jesus said to Peter when he was asking about John: "What is that to you? You follow me!" (John 21:22).

The important thing, surely, is to believe that prayer is worthwhile; that there is Someone there who is inviting us into a relationship; and that even when it feels as if nothing is happening, the relationship exists. There is Someone there. If we follow him in our hearts, then it is to his heart that we will be drawn, and from there he opens to us the joys and the bliss of heaven. Our task is to bring heaven to earth, and make earth like heaven: "Thy will be done on earth as it is in heaven." Prayer is the key which unlocks the channels through which his Kingdom comes: and these channels are channels of deeper and deeper love. In the end, the result of prayer is love.

Stages in our prayer journey – (written 2023)
How we pray now is not necessarily how we will always pray. Much has been written about the development of the spiritual life in the context of religious life, and currently there are numerous books and articles about how to pray for those living busy lives outside a monastic setting.

We can go on retreats, days of recollection, meet up with a spiritual director or discuss spiritual things with a friend over coffee.

But I believe that little attention has been paid to the difficult 'space' in between the two worlds; our spiritual growth and sensibilities, and the 'outside' world where we have to engage ourselves and our brains and our actions in the very mundane world around us.

Yes – theologically we are encouraged to see God in all things. Of course.

But that is very different to making the transition from a very nourishing time of prayer, maybe, to engaging fully in our business affairs, meetings, calculations, engagement with all sorts of different practical and ideological situations.

How do we move from one mindset to the other? After a busy day at the office, or the school, or whatever, all we may want to do is relax at home and engage with the entirely practical and domestic side of things – although these also pose numerous problems and stresses. Or we may want to disengage and retreat into prayer, but that is not always possible. Our children may be clamouring for attention; our wives or husbands may need us. We may well have to postpone our quiet and reflective time until later. Or maybe our only way of gaining some 'me-time' is to go out running or engage in some kind of sport or take the dog for a walk. Returning to nature and experiencing its healing power is being rediscovered. We may experience a deep longing for the nourishment of real prayer. It is interesting how many people resort to listening on earphones – possibly to music – in order to escape the overstimulation of the outside world.

But it works the other way too. When we are having a satisfying and happy day in ordinary activities, we may feel strangely reluctant to switch on our 'spiritual side' and engage in deep reflection or prayer. We may even resent the amount of time it takes when there is so little time available to be spread around so many pressing - and authentic - engagements and activities. There is a double grief that needs to be worked through and managed. Firstly, when we have to tear ourselves away from situations where we are experiencing spiritual nourishment and peace. Secondly, when we have to tear ourselves away from family and domestic and work activities to engage in specifically 'spiritual' activity.

It is this transition from one 'world' to another that I want to explore. Once I wrote that there is a sort of 'spiritual epiglottis' inside us. As the physical epiglottis switches between opening the airway to our lungs and the route to our stomach, so the spiritual epiglottis switches our energy and perception from the spiritual way of thinking and experiencing, which is hopefully growing within us, to the practical living of our beliefs in our actual busy lives.

It does not seem possible to be aware, or to live, both ways at the same time. Later in life, there should hopefully be an integration of the two, but that may be much later, in old age, when the hustle and bustle usually subsides.

At any time on our journey: adolescence, retirement, old age: we may find ourselves tiring of the infinite number of words that abound in our life. If we read the Divine Office, it may all seem too much. Actual participation in the liturgy in the church, for example, as a reader, may feel like a distraction. We are attracted and drawn into a more contemplative, wordless, form of prayer. Do not be afraid or troubled by this. Commit it all to the guidance of the Holy Spirit: it is all part of the journey. And, like all the stages, it is not permanent. The experience will be absorbed into our growth and serve as a resource through the rest of our life.

We are not alone in this ongoing process of our transformation. What I have not mentioned is the enormous power and strength of the sacraments. These feed and nourish both our spiritual growth and also our bodies and practical lives. So much can be said: explore and ponder it yourself! I find it helpful to consider not so much what the Eucharistic sacrifice is , but what it does; the effect in our lives and the life of the world itself. But that is a whole different topic.

To return to our journey: providential circumstances often help us.

The old spiritual writings speak of a time of purgation. This is a reality, probably, for all of us. It may come in the form of an illness or an injury or disability or it may be we are called on to care for someone else close to us. This will rock us out of our normal pursuits. We have deeper emotions to cope with. We have to adapt our lifestyle to accommodate the new responsibilities and limitations. We may have to cope with pain. We undoubtedly have to learn to waive our own plans and intentions and give preference to the needs we are experiencing. This must all equate with the training of the will written about in the classics. We have to learn to cope with difficult people and unreasonable demands, often give up cherished dreams, and learn how to be helpless and inadequate. This all throws us more and more deeply into the arms of the Lord, asking for his strength to help us to cope.

And he responds!

Gradually we may find the way to be courageous and not to give way to feelings of despair. Gradually we may even find a new freedom in the situation given to us.

The path of illumination is in some ways even more difficult to integrate into our growth and being. It may even be more difficult for those around us too! If we are totally taken up with a new experience of the Holy Spirit, it can be quite overwhelming. Those we work with may find it bewildering, to say the least. The family may find it very trying if they have not experienced anything like it themselves. We also may find ourselves unable to concentrate on anything else for a time.

Oh wow!

And then, after maybe some years later, when everything has settled down, and even when any mission that we feel we have been called to undertake has been more or less completed, there may come a time of stark aridity.

This is hard to take. What has happened? Where have all the comforting prayer experiences gone? Maybe I can only just kneel down and cry out 'Help!' or 'Lord, have mercy!'

Was it all a dream? Yet somehow, if we persevere, we begin to realise that there is a deep meaning even in this experience. One sign of its authenticity in the context of our spiritual journey is that, at heart, we do not really want to change the situation. We instinctively recognise that there is something to be learned from this experience.

In all this, an understanding director or a spiritual friend or helpful books can be invaluable.

This dryness may last for years. But it is an opportunity to engage our rational, thinking self. We can read more widely, we can challenge and think through many doctrines and opinions that we have previously taken for granted. We can maybe 're-learn' the language of the world – catch up with young people and learn how they think and speak and what their values are; listen to their views and discover where they are 'coming from'. It can be a very fruitful and fulfilling time. It may really encourage us when we experience how much goodness, creativity, and care for others abound in our so-called 'secular' world.

It is a tragedy when people get stuck in this stage and claim they have 'lost their faith'.

At last, as the tide slowly but surely fills an estuary and the dry reeds begin to soak up the water and become flexible once more, we begin to find an integration in ourselves. Our centre seems to have descended to a level beneath the struggles, joy and sorrows of previous years, and we find ourselves at last content and at peace.

So we come at long last to the precious haven of old age. This is often accompanied by physical – or mental – infirmity. But hopefully it is a time for reflection on our lives. At last we have time to look back and ponder our actions, our relationships, our life's journey. We may find time to speak more deeply with close members of our family. We may learn to see things we have taken for granted with a different perspective and learn facts of which we were unaware at the time.

If we are brave we can clear out material from the past – writings, memorabilia – so that we can travel less encumbered towards the ultimate end of our human lives. We learn to achieve a balance in our lives, giving space to all aspects of our being. And at last we may find that our inner thinking is mirrored in, or can be expressed through, our outer ways of thinking, speaking and acting.

We can begin to embrace yet another New Beginning, when all will at last make sense.

8. Difficulties

I want to explore just a little the place of the cross in prayer. Jesus said that devils are removed (and recognised) through prayer and fasting, and in the tradition of the church, prayer is always linked with fasting, or penance. Only in our time do we speak of prayer quite frequently without specific mention of fasting.

This may be because we are exploring the positive aspects of the prayer relationship, and do not want to dwell on the so-called negative side. But let's consider: if you have been at a church meeting, and no one put the chairs back afterwards, and then you noticed the dirty tea-towels which needed to be taken home and washed by someone, and then the door wouldn't lock because the key kept jamming, and you had to get another key from the minister, and eventually you got home really late and you flopped into a chair with a cup of tea ... did you not feel in your heart of hearts that somehow the Lord was specially with you?

If you have responded to the call of a neighbour in need which took time and energy and emotions that you felt you simply did not have, but which somehow you found, or were given ... did you not feel especially close to him?

How can we expect our prayer to deepen and expand in meaning, or our relationship with him to progress, if we do not join him in hardship? St. Ignatius speaks of the Lord's invitation to be with him as the invitation of a king going out to battle. We are invited to share with the king the hardships of the fight: sleeping on rough ground, losing sleep, low provisions, danger, wounds and weariness. But as we have shared in the hardships, so we are also invited to share the spoils of victory with him, and to share the rewards of peace and happiness afterwards. If we have been with him in the hardships of the battle, we will share in the joy and the honours of victory.

If we are not in some way sharing the hardships, which are where he is, how can we relate to him in prayer? Surely we are in a different place from where he is; we are sitting at home while he is out on the field. No wonder we have to raise our voice for him to hear — we are too far away from him!

You will see that I have equated the service and hardships of ordinary life with Christian penance and fasting. That is because I believe that, for most of us, that is where the real hardships come. If we are called to lay life, then it is in the stuff and fabric of our lay life that we encounter both the cross and the resurrection. We 'offer up' our days and all that we do in them — the joys and the sorrows, the pain and the pleasure — and in linking them to the cross, passion and resurrection of Jesus, they become fruitful and are given deeper meaning.

Some people, for example, those who are contemplatives in an enclosed order, are doing something different. They are witnessing to a resurrection through death in a very specific way. They voluntarily renounce all that belongs to human life and freedom in order to be given back a truer life, so that their sacrifice, linked to the death of Jesus, may also "win great hordes for his tribute". They are invited to this vocation by God; it is accomplished in God. It is deeply mysterious: the only 'proof' is that it works. Some contemplatives are among the most complete, full, joyous human beings that one can ever meet anywhere. Thousands testify to the efficacy of the prayer of the contemplative communities.

As some are called to share specifically in Jesus' ministries of baptising, of teaching, of healing, of priesthood, even though all pertain to all Christians, so some are called more specifically to share in his work of redemptive suffering, though we are all asked to 'carry our cross'. This includes the special mission of the sick and the handicapped: even though God never wanted anyone to be ill or disabled, linked with Jesus' death, such suffering can be fruitful, and can release channels of grace to an unbelieving society. He has invited our small efforts to be joined with his in all aspects of his great work of redeeming the world and bringing all into union with God, in Christ, through the Spirit.

Most of us will find that we lie between the two extremes of fully active life and fully contemplative life, but it is in that context that we should, I think, consider the question of penance.

Prayer, fasting and almsgiving are the traditional recommendations of the Church. The last is the easiest to speak about: giving alms is giving to those in need, and deeper and deeper giving is a sure way of the cross. So the giving extends not just to money, but to time, to energy, to attention — but, take heart! We can never outdo God in generosity! The more we give, the more we receive. To give in accordance with the heart of Christ is an art and a skill. We can be tempted to give too much. He always graciously accepts it. He never makes us feel foolish. But he may gently point out considerations of prudence. Most saints started off by going to extremes. Later, a moderation set in, which is not to be despised. Their real martyrdoms came in ways, as they always do, which they had not chosen.

The difficulty with giving too much is that it may harm us, by frightening us. We may think: this is too much for me! I cannot keep it up. I can't keep going to all these meetings, and doing so much. I'm not good enough, obviously. So we class ourselves as 'not meant for it' and may even stop going to church. I've met many people who are afraid to go to church because of all the demands put on them: demands to give, demands to do. That is not God doing it: it is other people, and ourselves agreeing to it. We are called to give, yes, but gently, at our own pace of growth. God lays it gently on us. We are stretched, but not torn. We are given, not wrenched apart. Only if we are called to go through a real crucifixion is violence done to us, but then it feels different: we are in circumstances beyond our control. Our only choice is to do as best we can in a situation not of our choosing (though maybe as a result of our choices). So — don't accept being a martyr too easily! We do not choose our own cross; when it comes, it is laid on us in an inescapable way. That is part of the 'cross-ness' of it. For the greater part of Christian life, it is a question of finding the pace of the Spirit working in us, and aligning ourselves with this, so that our lives proclaim both the cross and the resurrection. The resurrection, the triumph of good over evil, of joy over sorrow, is just as important a message for our time.

How can we show this message if we ignore the sorrow? We are back to the question of penance.

There are three aspects of this (at least). One is the aspect of voluntary self-denial. This may be giving up sugar in Lent, or biscuits, or sweets, or some television or whatever. This is by way of training our will. Instead of having our hearts set on something — "I can't possibly manage without that" — we find we achieve a new mastery over it in that we have given it up for a time and are now free to take it or leave it. With increased mastery over such things, our areas of choice expand — we become more free. There are more areas in which the Spirit can now be effective. By training ourselves in little things, we are more able to make bigger decisions in accordance with the will of God.

The second aspect is the one we have already considered: the hardships can be offered to God, in Christ, as part of the "making up in my own body what is missing from the sufferings of Christ" (Col. 1:24) for the redemption of the world.

The last aspect is something a bit different. I think we are very shy about talking about punishment for wrong-doing these days. This is partly in reaction to an over judgmental attitude in the past. It is partly due to a greater understanding of what makes people do wrong in the first place, and a desire to heal rather than to punish, which is good. But we are in danger of losing out on something which can be helpful.

We have an innate sense of justice, of right and wrong. Why do most cops and robbers stories end with the robber being caught? Whether such stories are set with American police, British police, space fiction heroes or whatever, we nevertheless require that the 'goodies' win, and that the 'baddies' don't get away with it.

Another place where this is very obvious is at wrestling matches: people shout for the 'goodie', yell at the 'baddie', and insist on satisfaction — often in terms of another encounter (at a later date) if the baddie happens to win.

"Except you become as little children..." Children understand this well. If they have done wrong, they expect to be punished. If the punishment is fair, then they feel right again afterwards.

Suppose we have done something wrong. It is all right to be told that recompense has been made on the cross; that we have been forgiven. It is all right that we know that nothing we do can in fact make up to a holy God for that sin; that all is grace and only by relying completely on Jesus can the way back to union with God be opened. Our human mind still needs to fasten on to something to make it 'feel' all right. If we really repent, at depth, with tears — then that can 'do the trick'. What if we deprive ourselves of something we like as a punishment? What if we suggest to ourselves something that we can do as a means of making amends? Is that not taking our humanity seriously, and actually helping us to take in that we should not have done what we did? It means committing ourselves to the fact that what we did was wrong. It means trying seriously to prevent ourselves from doing it again. It means taking our repentance off the 'spiritual' level and making it a fact in our human, actual life as well. It means recognising that we are not too old to do things wrong and have to be punished.

That can be a shock to some people. It has become too easy to know that Christ did it all for us on the cross. We have lost all sense of what we have been saved from. Of course, anything we do is quite inadequate, but I believe it is psychologically important that we do something. What we do is almost irrelevant. It is the attitude in which we do it that is important.

Such acts and attitudes add strength to our prayer, and realism to our growth. But again, it is not for us to decide what to do in our own self-sufficiency and arrogance. We come humbly to our God, express our willingness to explore these areas, and ask him to lead us and help us. Then we are less likely to go astray.

Any growth in the Christian life should result in greater freedom. Many of us nevertheless feel trapped. It may be helpful to look at some of our prisons — remembering all the time that many Christians are literally in prisons for their faith. So what do our prisons look like? Some of them are connected with our physical nature, though not made of bricks. They may be made of timetables; or of various demands made on us: having to give the children a lift to wherever they are going because it is not safe for them to go alone; having to miss our lunch hour because a certain piece of work has to be completed in order to catch the post which has to go at a certain time. We have to prepare meals because we have to eat. Commitments, timetables, deadlines, all trap us and leave us crying to be free.

It helps to recognise that there is a problem. These prison walls are wrong! But the practical answer is, as far as I can see, contained in the old dictum: 'What can't be cured must be endured'. First we look to see if anything can be changed to let us out of our prison. (That can actually be a very real way of praying, with quite remarkable results. Release me from this trap! God is the one who releases the bird from the snare of the fowler.) But if there is no way of release, then a willing acceptance of the situation can ease the distress. It is the principle contained in the admonition to turn the other cheek or to go the second mile. Don't fight it. Acceptance brings a sense of freedom because we have freely chosen, with our own will, to accept what is given to us (even if it is wrongly given). It sometimes seems like cowardice not to fight it, but acceptance can bring peace. I suspect the art lies in knowing when to fight and when to surrender! Often our only choice is whether or not we do the inevitable willingly and cheerfully, or not. Always, the request for the extra mile is unjust, unfair. Always, we are tempted to resentment. Always, joy and peace come in willing acceptance.

There are other freedoms. The freedom of the mind is equally important. This is to do with Truth. We need accurate facts and also a mind free from prejudice in order to listen, understand, reflect, and learn. The prisons of the mind are just as confining as the prisons of the body.

When the mind is exploring Truth it can feel wonderfully free. St. Ignatius said that the mind absorbs truth like a sponge absorbing water; falsehood is like water dripping on a stone, and spitting off. But how do we actually get free of prejudice? How do we get an open mind? Again, I believe it is a gift from God, but one he wants to give us. We can ask for it in prayer. When we are willing to release our old opinions, then openness can be given. We need grace even for that willingness; but when it is given, and we do release, then we find that our beliefs are given back to us in renewed form. We never really lose anything. If only we could trust him to keep safe for us the precious things we hold, then we would not need to grab them and hold on to them defensively. Even memories ... if we let memories go, then they grow and are given back to us. The bereaved person who keeps the room of the deceased untouched for years is depriving themselves of a real present relationship, in their clinging to the past. The parent who insists on keeping their child as a child does the same — we know this. But it is hard to avoid, and we do need help. Once again, it is the principle of the cross; of death and resurrection: death of old opinions; resurrection based in old beliefs and relationships, found again in a new way.

Freedom from conditioning from the past is another area which can be brought into our prayer. Even if the conditioning is good, to be free we need to re-examine it and embrace it for ourselves, rather than following old methods rigidly, by rote. Rote or habit can be excellent as a modus vivendi; a way of saving energy, so that we do not have to think out methods every time we do something. But from time to time there is definitely a case for reassessing and re-examining what we do and why we do it.

If we pray for release from the restrictions in our minds, then we should pray also to recognise the challenges that are sent to us which will enable these changes. Prejudices are sometimes dispelled through circumstances: for instance, a new relationship. Our part is to allow such a relationship a chance to develop. Answers to prayer can come in very unexpected ways. We need to be able to recognise the openings which will challenge us, and learn to respond.

We may need to be released from our self-image. Perhaps we find ourselves impossible to live up to, or, at the least, very demanding. It can sometimes be most liberating when we allow ourselves, for instance, to make mistakes. We may come to realise that it doesn't really matter, except where our self-image is concerned.

By learning to release things (or people) we find that we have freed them to be themselves, and freed our will to make right decisions. As a compass can only find the right direction when there is no other metal around to attract it and distort it, so our will needs to be detached from 'musts' in our lives, in order to choose properly and freely. Some obligations are, of course, real obligations — but perhaps not as many and in not the same way as we sometimes think. These real obligations, or 'givens', provide the context in which our free decisions are made.

Our 'yes' to God is so often made up of many tiny, insignificant 'yes's', the sum total of which constitute our way to heaven.

Each one of these 'yes's' costs something; some will amount to real sacrifice. But that is what it is all about.

9. Church Community Life

For most of us, our Christian life is centred on the parish or church community, and this is our spiritual base. It is there we celebrate Christmas and Easter and our own family occasions, and there above all that we want to feel at home. It is in that context that our path to heaven is forged. Parish or other community life can be both joyful and frustrating; intensely hurtful, and deeply comforting. It is where we learn to live with other people whom otherwise we would never meet. It is in a real sense our 'extended family', or even our only family. It brings us very real challenges and very real rewards.

Part of the challenge lies in mixing with all sorts of different people in a very personal way: people we are asked to love. "See how these Christians love one another" is a constant spur to proper behaviour which will not go away. So when things go wrong, as they always do, in all denominations, we feel doubly ashamed. It may even be because we are trying so hard and not letting irritation and frustration surface, that things sometimes go so drastically wrong.

All denominations in recent years have had to face major changes, partly arising from the problem of relating old traditions to a modern world: a world of technology, a world of television, a world of fast communications across its surface, and, in this country at least, a world where most people have had a reasonable education one way or another.

In the Church of England there has been the move from the Book of Common Prayer to Common Worship: from an emphasis mainly on Matins and Evensong to a greater place for the Parish Communion. The Roman Catholic Church has faced up to the challenge both in producing the Vatican II documents and in implementing them. All churches have a renewed emphasis on healing. The Congregationalists and Presbyterians united to become the United Reformed Church; the Methodists brought in a new hymn book.

Many of these changes mark a move from a more individualist approach to a more community approach — and this is not always an easy move to make. In some cases it also marks a move from a more contemplative approach to a more participative and active one. This also can cause unease — as well as a great feeling of relief to those who like it. Are we right to call them 'old' and 'new'? Is there a place for both types of approach?

In ecumenism I find that people are still afraid that they will lose identity, lose their way of finding God, if the churches come together; that they will be part of an amorphous group engaging in mediocre, trying-to-please-everyone worship in which few will really feel at home. I think these fears should be taken seriously. They are too widespread and have lasted too long to be ignored. Part of the answer is to remember God's infinite love and care for the individual: each one of us is precious in his sight, and this implies consideration of individual needs. This is something that should never be lost sight of. In Isaiah it says God will bring us together from the four corners of the earth: that sounds like a very large ecumenical gathering! There is nothing to say that our individuality is lost. So the challenge is: how do we preserve identity and variety in unity?

The model is, of course, in the Trinity itself: three persons in one. This is the source of our variety, and the model for unity in variety. Worship, or ways of being Christian, can focus on any aspect or all aspects of the Trinity; that is why we should expect to find differences. We have already considered the two-way dynamic of the Christian life — in the words of Teilhard de Chardin, the growth and the renunciation: the movement outward, exploring the world, and discovering God active in the world; the movement inward, back into ourselves, to reflect, ponder, interpret, worship, to find God also within ourselves. We can't physically do both at the same time! They are different phases in our prayer life

As we look at the world, we cannot but see its infinite variety, in an overall unity. The plural nature of today's world is taken for granted. A particular example of this is something like a forest or a garden: thousands and thousands of uniquely different components go into making the overall reality.

So it is in the church. Our important task, as individuals, is to seek the Lord and his way for us. This applies also to a congregation: what is our special charism? What are we offering to the total church life? And also our denomination? What is our special gift or mark that we want to offer or hold in trust for the whole church?

To return to the individual: to find the Lord's way for me does not mean choosing a corner and digging in and refusing to hear anyone else: it means keeping my mind open and trying different things — for example, different ways of prayer, different books, different people. But it does mean a growing sensitivity to what is right for me now, at this stage of my Christian growth and development, and a growing confidence in choosing just one of the many ways without being bewildered and threatened by what other people may be doing, which is different. And this means also that we will be more able to listen and understand their different point of view.

Trying different things to discover what is helpful does not mean indulging in a sort of 'dilettantism'; a sort of butterfly approach that sips the best from all traditions but will never settle and become part of the daily toil and growth which produces that 'best'. But we do have an overall church that produces variety, and that is a great gift, one to be used and treasured properly. Enjoying the variety is one aspect; working to produce one part of that variety is another role. I see no reason why any part should be lost! We bring our gifts and share them with each other, or use them on behalf of each other. Such gifts are given to the church as a whole, which includes us, and we should all rejoice over them.

Is there a limit to variety? Well, yes, I think so, but probably not nearly so tight as we may imagine.

This idea of having confidence in one's own way of prayer and worship in the face of variety is shown again if we consider ways of service. There are so many good causes: prisoners of conscience, victims of oppression, torture, war all over the world, Shelter, social security reform; rights of unborn children, retreat work, education; inter-faith dialogue, etc., etc., etc. We can be bombarded with good causes to which we are asked to respond.

The same principle can apply that we have been thinking about. We need to return to the Lord in our own personal prayer, and try to discern (with help if need be) the causes or areas of service, perhaps only one or two, that we are being asked to help with, and to work out in prayer and practice, by trial and error, the extent of our commitment - commitment which may stretch us, but does not harass and distress us, and is not at the expense of too many other duties and commitments: a commitment with which we are, at depth, at peace.

Then we thank God that there are other people called to minister to the other needs that we cannot do anything about.

It is only because of today's improvements in communications and awareness that we have this problem of too much information and too many requests; but it can destroy our joy and peace in the Lord.

As we grow in confidence in our own way and our special way of serving in the church, we will not be threatened by what other people do and how they see things. But that still may not be the end of our problems. We need to be strong enough to be able to say 'no' regretfully to requests for help where it is going to push us too far, and also to understand when people refuse us the help for which we are asking. It may be that the church itself is over-extending itself.

The opposite problem is when people feel they are simply not being asked, or that their help is not wanted. This again is where genuine love comes into play. Those who are helping need to take on the prospective helper and show them the ropes patiently, at a pace they can absorb, and to find them something which they really can do. It also means accepting sometimes jobs done less than perfectly: a constant balance between wanting the best for the house of the Lord, and accepting the gifts which people are able to offer. Should we exclude anyone from offering? The widow's mite may be a hymn sung out of tune, but still infinitely precious to the Lord. The problem really bites when the less-than-perfect help interferes with the real substance of the worship, as with a bad reader who is incomprehensible or inaudible. I am not saying that there are no limits to tolerance!

Kind compromise is to me a Christian solution. But the principle remains the same: that we should all do our best to see that everyone is able to offer some service, if they wish.

Every denomination and, I think, every parish works on a checks-and-balances system. We all have power people, authority people, pressure groups, a general feeling of the mind of the people which cannot be abused. And, whatever our theology, a determined person can always work the system, and exercise a certain amount of power regardless of where the authority lies. It may be that this will always be necessary as a means of getting good things done.

But the exercise of power can become a way of life: it can be abused in the hands of certain people. It can give rise to self-aggrandisement and self-seeking, or cause jealousy among others. It can mean that, whatever other needs or pressures are around, I am going to make sure that I have things done my way. My need to be involved and to be important is the most important thing in my life: it must be insisted on by whatever means are available, and other people must be made to give way.

Is this really what we want? And particularly, is this what we want in Christ's church? When things go wrong, we cannot just blame the system: the responsibility always belongs to individuals within it, and they can include us. What is needed is a conversion of heart — for all of us, at an ever-deepening level.

As human beings we have very deep needs: the need to be accepted; the need to belong; the need to be able to contribute; the need to be known. Most of the unedifying and petty power struggles which we see going on in all areas of life are the expression of one or other of these needs not being recognised and showing itself in the wrong way. We need to ask our Lord to help and heal us; ask him to satisfy us with love at these deep levels of our being. Then lesser loves and loyalties will not spoil our work but, rather, enhance it.

The pain of the rejection of our gifts is a major problem. We all need to learn how to graciously accept the gifts of others, even when we do not quite see their value. But we also need to learn not to feel hurt when no hurt was intended. It is the devil's marvellous way of stopping good people giving generously to the church — sooner or later you will be hurt. It happens in every church and every denomination that I have had anything to do with. It is painful, but we do ourselves far more harm if we let it make any difference to our attitude of generous giving.

We need to develop the attitude of rejoicing in gifts given to others, because God has given them for our benefit, for the good of his church, for the good of the world. That is the end of power-struggling. We are talking about a love that seeks not its own, but rejoices in goodness wherever it is found. We are talking about an attitude that can see only God in his goodness in all the good gifts that he has given and does not mind which individual or which church has received the gift, so long as it is used generously for all. We are talking of an attitude that takes no account of honour or status or being recognised, because it recognises that Jesus was often taken for a fool and had none of these things and sees no reason why things should be different for his followers.

The church, the community of believers, the community of those who love each other, should be the foretaste on earth of the joys of heaven. In the church we should find par excellence humility and joyful, non-patronising sharing and receiving of each other's gifts and talents and service. We should be showing others how power and authority, at whatever level, when exercised by people in loving relationships with each other, result in mutual growth and yield much fruit, to the glory of our Lord and Master, Jesus Christ, to whom we are all accountable. It is a goal and a grace to be continually worked for and prayed for — surely he will hear and answer our prayer.

"Make real friends with the poor" (Rom. 12:16 — Jerusalem Bible)

There are no class distinctions in Christ, but this can become a challenge in a parish. If we are called to be open with each other, to be real friends with each other and love one another, then somehow we must learn to relate to all people whether they are from 'better' or 'worse' backgrounds than ourselves. This is a two-way challenge. I may have to learn not to resent it when my neighbour in the parish has a new car, or expensive holidays, or a good place in the local private residential home. My neighbour must learn to work as an equal with people of lesser ability, offering their gifts in a manner that will be acceptable. When I was helping to serve soup to vagrants on one occasion, it was bitingly cold. I wanted to wear my new coat for warmth. Surely they had to accept me with my new coat, the same as I had to accept them as I found them.

In a parish we all mix in together in a way unprecedented in other situations. Because it is so challenging, some of us may want to duck out and keep up the barriers: the result of this is unfriendly and unwelcoming congregations, or cliques within congregations.

But let us not underestimate the challenges. If I am a real friend with someone, and they are receiving financial assistance from the State, and through reasons not of their own making (or even of their own making) owe, say, £2,000 on credit cards and are being crushed by the burden and worry of it ... how do I respond? Can I really say it is none of my affair? But if I admit to being involved, then I am called on somehow to help. I may well be called in to enter into the problems and difficulties of a life I had never imagined could be lived that way. Or if a family I know breaks up, what are my responsibilities towards the children, or either partner? It is too easy to say that it is too difficult a situation for me to be involved in. Of course, professional help is available and is often really helpful. Of course, well-meaning but inexpert people can cause a lot of pain by insensitive advice. But that does not mean that there may not be something real that I can do and which I should do, even though it means 'getting involved', with perhaps a long-term commitment.

To be really open to people is one of the most challenging parts of the Gospel to live out. If you are known to be someone who doesn't mind helping, among the genuine requests will be many from those who live by exploiting others one way or another. There will be a continual tussle between help that has been promised and family or other commitments. There will be family who claim priority over all else, as well as family who share the vision and the desire to help. There will be 'phone calls at all sorts of times, often late at night, from people who are very difficult to cut short — not least because their needs are genuine. There will be people who have always been starved of love and who at last see you as the means of making up what they have missed — and they may be right. It is a long-term task, giving them the love and assurance necessary to help them stand on their own in relationships of true interdependence; and not letting them drain and suck all the energy from you. It means allowing them to call you unchristian when you do not immediately fall in with all they ask.

All this throws you right back in prayer to the Lord, and he is very near. This task of seeking and caring for the lost sheep, in all its inordinate amount of 'wasted' time and energy, is one very close to his heart. One experiences something of what it is to be eaten and devoured by the world, and yet in the heart of it all there can be a very deep peace. The ministries of listening and of hospitality are very important in today's church, when so many people around us are on their own or have never experienced proper family love. If we all were to take our share, no one person would be too over-burdened, and there would be no one who did not have their friend who would listen to them.

Of course, this is not the only ministry in the church. We have already thought about choosing one's own 'good cause' and not being distracted by trying to do everything. Good causes abound, but the challenges to the personality are much the same in all of them. I am again thinking of situations like arriving to start an event and finding that the hall is not open as promised and you have to chase around to find someone with a key; then the heat is not on; then the helper on whom you were relying comes late or not at all. A couple of helpers will be very deaf without hearing aids — and yet another will have been offended by someone or other in some place or other and want to tell you all about it; or worse, will have been offended by one of your other helpers and you have to spend time sorting it out. You keep your patience for 99% of the time and then someone catches you at just the wrong moment with something you have already explained and you sound a little short, and there is yet another upset. And yet at the end of the day, people will tell you how they enjoyed whatever it was, and there will be a real sense of fellowship among all the helpers, and somehow the seed that was sown in tears is reaped in joy.

Surely the sharing of these experiences and the bearing of the pinpricks are the very stuff of what church community life is about, and make up the road to sanctity for most of us.

One thing to beware of is a certain false pride. There is no point in complaining that no one has offered to help, and being too proud actually to ask for it. I know that the difficulty is that, often when you ask, the help is refused for various reasons, and you feel stupid and even 'pushy', but just sometimes the help is given and the person is delighted. For every one who says "No one offered" there is someone saying "No one asked me!" Or even, "No one ever asks me". Both 'sides' are right: of course people should see needs and offer, but most don't. Of course asking is tiring and even embarrassing, but I am sure we should persevere one way or another — while always being happy to accept a negative answer graciously and promptly. Nothing is more damaging than people being afraid to come to church because they get set on! But I have heard that the last gift of the Holy Spirit is a thick skin.

This question of being honest with ourselves and asking for help when we need it can apply to things like bus or car expenses, or help with an inflated-by-church-calls 'phone bill. These things can be a constant niggling worry which can easily turn to resentment and spoil our joy in what we are doing. There are surely others in the church community who would like to help but for various reasons cannot be actively involved: they may be pleased to help in small financial ways. It may be that this is their way of participating, and if we do not let them, we are keeping them out. A good rule is that, if something persists as a cause of resentment, something drastic should be done. It is no good wishing that things were different. Humility exists in recognising that we are as we are with all our particular circumstances, and asking for help when we need it is the sensible and logical consequence.

Having said all this, there will always be problems working in a parish or other church community. The best defence is to keep a level head and as happy a life as possible outside it: then there will be some possibility of keeping a sense of proportion. If we have the parish as our only interest and our entire life, then hurts and slights will assume exaggerated importance. There can also be a danger of losing touch with the world outside.

Many of us will have jobs and family and friends and possibly even hobbies. Even if we haven't, if we live alone and are not working, it is still a good idea to have some contacts and friends and activities quite apart from parish life. We are told in the documents of Vatican II that our vocation as lay people is to bring our Christianity to the world: to bring our standards and our thinking and our love and our interpretation of the meaning of life to all that we meet and do, and thus transform them into Christ's new Creation. This cannot be done if we are not actually meeting and living and participating in the affairs of the world and the lives of other people.

We may well not be called to overt evangelism, but the call to be Christ in the world is the call of every baptised Christian. It is the work of a lifetime. How do we set about it? Only by deepening our own life in Christ. Our motivation is not our own sanctification: it is that we may be more perfectly the people he wants us to be, so that those who do not know him may see and experience something of his love and care and meaning, and come to know him too. How many of those who have rejected church and Christianity have done so for the best possible motives? Have done so because the Christ they perceived in us was less than the Christ they hoped for and aspired to? Because the love they experienced in the church was less than the love they experienced outside it? Yes, the church is a church of sinners and it is unfair to expect instant goodness on the part of all those who belong; but it is also unfair of us not to make every possible effort to be the best possible version of ourselves, in Christ, that we can be, for the sake of those who seek and have not yet found.

The Sacraments
Many people find that one of the greatest blessings of the church comes through receiving the sacraments, especially Baptism and the Eucharist.

As we are called to be full human beings, in harmony with God, through Christ and the Holy Spirit, so the sacrament of the Eucharist feeds and nourishes all aspects of our being, body and soul: both our interior and our exterior lives. Not an atom of ourselves is left out! Our gifts and talents are all fed and nourished and enabled to express themselves fully as and when the opportunities in our damaged world allow. And it is the damage, both inside and outside us, which creates the problems.

But adversity prompts us to exercise courage, resilience, innovation, creativity and a growing dependence on the Lord. We learn to experience the deeper values of hope, that enables us to keep going; faith, which encourages us to believe and think beyond the obvious, and charity which directs our attention away from ourselves. We begin to realise that we are one among countless others – a social and community being, though loved individually. We are part of the very Body of Christ.

10. Exile

I do not think we take nearly seriously enough the fact that we live outside the Garden: that we are living in exile. Exile was a favourite theme of former generations: a Catholic prayer to Mary refers to us as "poor, banished children of Eve, mourning and weeping in this vale of tears"; the hymn "O come, O come Emmanuel" speaks of our "lonely exile here". Today the idea seems less popular. Perhaps this is a good thing: bold confidence in the Spirit, sounding a clarion call to the world, is not an image to be lightly discarded. The incarnation of Jesus altered the position for all time. Yet how do we explain the yearning for something more that we sometimes experience in our poetic moods? What is the elusive quality which seems just beyond our grasp? Why is it that satisfaction never quite fulfils? What is the vague unease which makes us ask, in the middle of beauty, "But is this really all?"

The Welsh have a word, 'hiraeth', which expresses this nameless longing and yearning for a homeland. And what ailed Keats' knight-at-arms "alone and palely loitering" if it was not the taste of something beyond, something so utterly beautiful, something appealing to senses so beyond the human senses, that all was pale and dry, lifeless, following the experience? Natural mystics speak of a world of heightened perception. St. Teresa of Avila hints at heavenly music which is as much beyond earthly music as heaven is beyond earth.

Physically we can feel satisfied, replete. In our human spirit, we can also feel 'replete' in the right company, or with music, or art. But is there not a deeper, deep heart, which yearns, rightly, for more? The most beautiful description of this that I know is in C.S.Lewis' Narnia series: his description of the Land of Bism in The Silver Chair.

St. John of the Cross speaks of the loss of interest and pleasure in all worldly pleasures (legitimate pleasures) which he had experienced; a tastelessness in everything, following the rich taste of God.

All humankind hankers at depth after the taste of God in real and deep contemplation. Does that mean that we are left in hopelessness, destined to an ever deeper, largely unsatisfied thirst, which is never properly slaked, but is sufficient to spoil our enjoyment of all else? Or which, having been tasted, leaves us listless forever?

Some people genuinely do get stuck here. There is a renewal, both within and without the church. Many people have direct experience of spiritual things, but this does not help everybody to lead a full and happier life as a result.

Of course, space must be left for meditation and contemplation — but how does one navigate the passage back out into the outside world? How does one leave the Garden? How much truth is there in the story of Orpheus and Euridyce, that if you look back on the way out, you lose all that you have gained?

To change the analogy, it seems to me that many people get stuck in the line of breakers along the seashore. They have left the shallows, but not yet reached the deep beyond the breakers; or they have left the deep and never quite made it back to the shallows. They are buffeted on all sides, and quite unable to function.

The Christian answer to this lies in the incarnation: Christ left heaven to enter into human life, sanctify it, and bring it back in him to the Father in heaven. In terms of actual Christian living, it is not a once-and-for-all answer, or even a theoretical one. The emptying out, the 'kenosis', the leaving heaven and all its joys to take on the limitations, and quieter joys, of being human, has to happen to us as often as we are also called to come apart with the Lord and share with him; to sup with him; to witness his transfiguration; to pray in him with the Father.

When we leave the mountain top to re-enter our ordinary mode of human life, it means we have to take on again the imperfections of our sinful human personality, not yet fully redeemed, and our life with all its unresolved problems. We have to re-enter a sinful world with sinful structures, into which we are drawn inevitably by our very shopping, talking and travelling. Even relationships with others may either draw us out and on into better versions of ourselves, or, alternatively, draw us into a level of action or conversation which we afterwards know to have been unworthy; less than appropriate to the person we glimpse we should or could be.

To leave his presence means to accept that we are going to get dirty, and to be willing for this to happen; knowing, of course, that the way back via sorrow and repentance is always open. There is no way of working in the vineyard without getting one's hands dirty. There is a lot of sound sense in "avoiding the occasion of sin", but for the wholehearted apostle this is not the same as refusing to enter into sinful situations with the intention of trying to help redeem them, but with one's eyes open as to the risk of being dirtied oneself by them.

Oh, the sadness of the sight of the person of prayer who is not prepared to take on the roughness of the cross, which began with the leaving of heaven and becoming human! Human life is to be embraced and loved wholeheartedly, as Jesus did; never to be despised.

The Holy Spirit is given to us to help us. It is Christ-in-us that enters these situations and Christ-in-us that heals them, if we are privileged to be of help. Contemplation in action means that Christ-in-us uncovers and reveals and makes to grow Christ in the world, in the Spirit. How, then, can we still say that we are exiles? Surely the experience of feeling an exile witnesses to the truth that our permanent setting is not here. We are living in the penultimate, not the ultimate. To the extent that we perceive this truth, we experience pain. For us, the situation and the experience are always made more painful by sin: it is not being in the world, and outside heaven, that causes the real hurt, but what that world can do: the bad atmospheres, the grasping, the sheer ugliness of greed, ambition and selfishness. These all constitute the sort of surround that makes our spirit literally faint within us.

If it is Christ-in-us that ministers to the world, then we must share also in his experience, and he surely must have felt this absence from heaven, even though he was God. The extreme of this was his cry of dereliction: he experienced the isolation, abandonment, alienation, of being cut off as though he also had sinned.

So, the exile of sin is real. No one knows how exile would feel without sin: without personal sin in ourselves and without sin in all the world around us. For contemplation in action to be complete it is necessary to have the cooperation of all creation: hence the hope and promise of a new Heaven and a new Earth. Only then will our complex nature feel at home and at rest in all its modes of being.

The ripping of the temple veil signified the way was once again open to the Holy of Holies. In the Holy Spirit, the way back into the garden was free once more. No angels barred the way: angels announced the news. The fruits of the trees of life and knowledge are given to us. But the Christian is not allowed to stay there. For the sake of those outside the garden, he or she takes on voluntary exile with all its joy and pain — and plants gardens wherever he or she goes.

One practical implication is that we may need two languages: one for inside the garden, and one for outside. Inside, you can speak freely in intimacy, heart to heart, spirit with spirit. Outside, you speak with people with hurt hearts, or hard hearts; with spirits crushed or hidden. If they will not communicate their hurt (and why should they, until they know you and trust you?), how can you speak? You have first to learn their language — often the language of unbelief. You have to identify the points of value in what they say, and build on that; and often learn from it in the process. You cannot impose your language and beliefs: you must learn first where they are.

Here are some starting-points. Most people have some idea of the value of a human being; or of the joy experienced in making something; or of the beauty of creation (perhaps from nature programmes on television); or of the joy and difficulties of parenthood. These are all ways in. Like the Lord, we have to pick out the homely and other values which are in fact held, and make them into parables to point the way to the Kingdom. But afterwards, we need to come back and converse in our own language of belief, with our companions on the way, so that we also continue to believe. It is so easy to use one language or the other; so very difficult to be at home in both, whilst retaining the same values.

It is often very satisfying working for the church. You can work at full stretch, the adrenalin flows, the Lord-in-you makes decisions, gives ideas, keeps you going ... and then! It comes to a stop.

Who are *you* — you when you are not working?

You have become a work-machine. You have 'lent' your brain and energy to the Lord, and you are suddenly returned to yourself, tired, spent. Where is your direction?

The interests and antennae have to be drawn back into yourself, right in, to face the opposite direction. He, the Lord, in silence and peace and passivity, he refreshes you. Ah, it is sweet.

And then, it is time to be turned inside out again, at depth. From the depths of your deep consolation, you have to be turned outwards, willingly, in love for the outside. You have to agree to serve without consolation or companion or result. The willingness must be total, even if the offer is never fully taken up; only so do you remain free.

It is the motif shown in the story of the three wise men: going out in all weathers, leaving what you have for the sake of what you do not see, because of a vision and a conviction, or even simply a hope. But it is a hope worth staking all on, because of the good it will bring, even though we may never experience it. Even if the hope were to be unfounded, it is worth staking all on it in case it might be true. That is total giving; then comes joy. There may also come companionship, consolation, and even results, but they must never be a condition of our response.

We are still left with the inherent suffering in a position where one is seeking to come closer to, and growing in longing for, a Lord who is increasingly attractive, in a situation where one must forever be leaving him, and serving him in absence and even in abandonment. Not that his Holy Spirit is niggardly in coming to us in service; it is simply that the sense of abandonment and grief is also part and parcel of the price of loving him. Many people speak of contemplation in action. It seems to me that this often means thinking about God in action, or acting in him, or allowing Christ-in-us to act. This is, of course, utterly appropriate to the Christian life, and should become more and more normal. But contemplation in action? Surely that is more than most of us could bear. Can we really bear to see the world as deeply as God sees it?

11. Evil and Suffering

Anyone who has had real contact with evil ceases to doubt in what we call devilry. There is a dimension beyond reason; a malignity which utterly repulses.

It is totally self-centred. There is a sameness about it, even in what is said by one person or another. The same arguments, the identical stands, are used by quite separate people. Personal identity is at its lowest ebb; all is subsumed in an impersonal force. It infects what it touches if defences are not kept up, and even then, it sullies, like mud. It ages, but not with the wisdom of maturity. This is real ageing; you feel older, tired, damaged. You feel old.

Evil has so many forms. It has its own version of everything that is good, and offers it as a substitute. So a right authority becomes tyranny; music becomes noise; beauty becomes shoddy and cheap attraction; love becomes lust for possession; striving and adventure become ruthless ambition and exploitation. The list is endless. But if you find anything you dislike or term as evil, look for the good, of which it is the corrupt form.

There is an activity about it. Try any really good enterprise and wait for the opposition. Usually the source is unexpected, and the form of the attack brings to mind words like 'sick', 'cheap', 'mean', 'dirty'. No wonder the writer of Genesis, seeking to explain this, writes of the curse of thistles and thorns which will always dog man's activity, as a means of punishment.

Another form of activity is the malign coming together of comparatively trivial circumstances which together make for a wrong far in excess of anything that any individual involved intended or even thought about.

Whatever name we give to it, the facts show evil to be around in a form that far exceeds our usual concepts of imperfection, incompleteness, growing pains or even ignorance. Sadly, there are also people and groups who deliberately encourage direct contact with evil.

On a wider scale, we see evil in institutions, large organisations, the very fabric of our social/political situation. Are these the powers and dominations of which St. Paul spoke?

If the mark of Christianity is love, so the mark of devilry is fear: fear that is possible at every level of personality down to the nadir of terror. To conquer fear is to learn to love; it is the way out of hell. The way out of hell is to love without thought of any return. Without thought of any return means that there is nothing that one is afraid to lose, not even the presence of a loved one. Even in the absence of the loved one, one carries on loving, utterly, at depth. There is pain, yes, but not fear. The acceptance of pain, in love, spells the end of fear.

But the fear has not been merely suppressed. It has been allowed out: expressed, felt, faced, and finally conquered through acceptance of the facts in the context of love.

After the Agony in the Garden, the pain was all to come, but the interior battle had been fought and won. Because of this, even the appalling dereliction and abandonment culminated in the cry: "Father, into your hands I commend my spirit."

Evil can damage in all sorts of ways. Many of these we can learn to overcome in ourselves. Objectively, it always involves cost in terms of time and energy. Oh, the amount of time these oppositions take to clear up or counter! Another trade mark is waste. The last word in some circumstances lies in physical force. When all else fails, brute force enters the arena; and people die.

Then things begin to change.

It is evil that supplies the flies on wounds inflicted in other ways. It is evil that loads the last straw. Grief can be born and expressed, and comfort found; where it is mixed with bitterness and resentment it is hurtful at all stages. Fatigue and low energy are not painful in themselves: it is the demands which take no account of them, the arguments and the tension, which make them painful. Even illness and pain are not too uncomfortable when one can actually give way to them. There are other factors which make them unbearable.

When we do not fight the unfairness of it all; when we do not chafe and fret; then we find that, in Christ, these things can be overcome. I am not saying that injustice and wrong should not be fought, but there is a time for active resistance and a time for passive acceptance which can be an even deeper form of resistance. To discern these times is an art and a skill, and a gift of the Spirit.

How do we understand the pain that could easily have been avoided? There are many times when we can say, "If only ... this" or "If only ... that", and whatever happened would not have happened. It leads one to suspect that there can be a reason for the pain in the very pain itself. And then you read the texts in Isaiah 52 and 53 and you think, yes, that refers to Christ's vicarious suffering for us and for the world. On him were laid the stripes that healed us all. If we share in his work and mission, then we may expect to share in his suffering work too. We are "baptised into his death and resurrection". How can we avoid suffering? All are invited to share in this work, although it does sometimes seem that some are specially chosen for a larger portion than others. Any value in it is for the sake of the salvation of the world. Suffering can never be an end in itself. Unless it is in the overall context of the mission, it is useless. It is part of the means to the end: the unity, in perfection, of all things, in Christ.

We are now speaking of a different dimension of suffering. Redemptive suffering, which neutralises and transforms, at root, at depth, the sin of the world and of us, is of a different nature from the ordinary accidents of life, the law of cause and effect, the suffering inherent in being human in an imperfect world. Redemptive suffering is perhaps the divine equivalent of our human idea of punishment. Expiation is the response to the divine which corresponds to human making of amends. Both elements are necessary for us to be restored to wholeness. These are the values to which the contemplative orders bear witness.

This whole mystery of suffering is the essence, the warp and woof, of the whole fabric of Christian and human living. Jesus understood his mission through reading and pondering the Old Testament scriptures. He explained the meaning of his passion and death to the disciples after the resurrection by explaining the scriptures. To understand a little more why the world is made so, we also could ponder the scriptures, particularly the Old Testament writings, and try to regain some sense of holiness, of the sin that separates us from it, and of the means of redemption.

So it is impossible to speak about Christianity without talking about the cross. It is mysteriously present whenever and wherever we scratch the surface of good and fruitful lives and action. We have only to look around at people we know, or at situations we have heard about. Wherever there is real evidence of the work of God, there is evidence also to be found of the cost that had to be paid, or of a personal preparation which led through paths involving suffering. It is apparent in the histories of all the great Christian figures. It is also what we are led to expect through the Gospel: if that is the way Jesus redeemed us, surely we, his followers and sharers in his continuing ministry, should expect the same conditions.

The cross is always a scandal; it is always wrong. Although it became the means of our redemption, the crucifixion was wrong: brutal, unjust, apparently unnecessary. Suffering is always a mystery, with no fully satisfactory answer for human beings. We may begin to glimpse an answer, but it can never be understood with ordinary reasoning. It is always a stumbling block, and often the reason why many do not find the 'narrow gate'. We are used to thinking about the actual crucifixion, but when we come across deep suffering in those we know, who have always tried to lead good lives, then we may often experience the problem and dilemma in much more real terms. The suffering of the innocent has always been deeply mysterious.

Suffering constitutes still the root paradox in Christianity: it makes a person's faith, or breaks it. Ultimately, I do not believe it is resolvable in this life — and certainly not in youth. As one gets older and looks back, one can begin to see clues as to where the meaning might lie — but only in hindsight, and only tentatively, so tentatively. Any explanation is inhuman, almost by definition.

The fact that Jesus suffered (and not just in his passion) indicates at least that he, or his Father, saw it as necessary to the resolution of the whole dilemma of human alienation from God as a result of sin. This particular dilemma is one whose true dimensions we are never, thank God, likely to see in this life. Contact with evil in separate incidents crushes most of us: the evil of Auschwitz; the evil in racism; the evil perceived in a totally self-centred and selfish person. The sight of all evil — its extent, its ramifications, its consequences, its depth — is mercifully hidden from us. How, then, can we hope to understand what is presented to us as not only its consequence, but its remedy?

Yet our own suffering can only begin to be understood within the grand scenario of creation, fall, redemption; together with the concept of growth, and a call to a destiny beyond our own capacities. In addition, we have to take into account the intimate connectedness of all creation; of ourselves with creation, of which we are a part, and of ourselves with our fellow beings all over the globe; the mutual bonds and interdependence in practical and deeper terms, of which twentieth-century individualism is only just dimly becoming aware. A later generation will wonder how we could have been so blind.

Ultimately, the answer to our deep suffering is the answer given to Job; to Mary; to Jesus himself. God's purposes, God's holiness, are mightily beyond us. We come to God in spite of them, not understanding them, and in our blindness show our trust and faith that he is good, in spite of all appearances to the contrary, and that we know (because of what we do know of him) that ultimately his purposes are good, and for our good.

Could Mary really have understood the reason for her suffering; her losing Jesus in Jerusalem; her pain during his public mission at hearing him called insane, and seeing his growing conflict with the authorities; her standing at the cross? Some of this pain could have been avoided by a few words from the right person at the right time. Jesus himself had to endure the sick beheading of John the Baptist; the sight of the squalor of the poor; the self-righteousness of some of the religious authorities; the lack of faith of those he hoped would know better. Surely he must have wondered what sort of world had been created and whether the end was really worth the pain. He would not have been human otherwise — and he was human.

It is too easy to write off the appalling offence of sin and evil, and God's outrage at seeing people suffer.

The only answer I know is to stand silent, and broken-hearted, before the omnipotence and omniscience of a holy God, knowing that this God is also a loving God, a passionately loving God, to an extent that we cannot begin to conceive; to lay ourselves, and our deep injuries, and our heart's complaints before him, without anger or resentment, because we have gone beyond both anger and resentment. And we stand, and we wait, for him to come to us; for him to speak, or touch. Not even to explain — simply, we have come to him because there is nowhere else to go.

And, at last, he comes; perhaps in calm silence, or in peace; in love; in reassurance; or even in the full flood of resurrection. Eventually, he comes, because that also is his nature and his pattern.

We underestimate the passionate desire of God that we also should be holy, perfect, as he is perfect. To achieve this he will go to any lengths. His salvific will is inexorable and total: anything, rather than that we should be lost. And, at the end, when we have seen why, then perhaps we also will say, "Yes, I am glad you did; I see now. Had I seen then as I do now, I would have wanted you to do, or allow, what you did."

12. Hell

Hell is both very difficult and very easy to think about. It is easy because it is always easy to imagine horrors and monstrosities; difficult, because mere horror is not what hell is about. The problem is hell in the context of a good and all-powerful God.

A further difficulty is that, if we give any real content to the question, if we really ponder it, then we are getting in touch with very primitive levels of fear and even terror in people: and that can be destructive. And yet: do we have the right not to consider it, when there are so very many references to it in the Bible? It is part of our Christian belief.

We should never consider hell except in the context of the mercy of God and the cross of Christ which keeps us from being there. Then we can dare to consider the doctrine; otherwise, we have to reduce it to something we find acceptable. Why consider it anyway? Because it says something about God's holiness and God's justice; and because the grace of fear of the consequences of evil brings humility into my love. I need to recognise that there is a problem. It is possible for me to mess up everything. A cheap salvation that relied for its teaching solely on the mercy of God would lose all sense of why the cross was necessary. Hell is terrifying; it is only against that backdrop that sacrifice and holocaust make any sense.

As we begin to realise the implications of what we have been saved from, so our love can move into thanksgiving and praise.

God never sends anyone to hell. It is the result of our own choices, and perhaps the more frightening because of it. You can plead with someone who sends you there, and they can change their minds and let you out. But if you are there as the result of your own continuing choices — refusal to love, refusal to trust, refusal to be forgiven, refusal to relate to people — and you are convinced you are incapable of choosing differently, or you do not want to choose differently for convincing reasons, then what hope is there?

The essence of hell is fear, because fear is the result of the absence of love. Fears originate from different levels and different causes. The deepest is a nameless terror which consumes one's being: fear of the void, of destruction, of non-being, of the withdrawal of love. But even to name it this far is to achieve some measure of control. Real terror is truly nameless, beyond the levels of concept. It is terror at the roots of our being; and being alone with it. It is seeing the depths of the abyss which sucks at our heels and threatens to draw us in forever. It is the stuff of which nightmares are made.

As lesser fears easily turn into anger, so deep fear turns into hate: twisting, tormenting, perverting hate; at worst, a hatred of innocence and of goodness, simply because they are lost to it. Such hate must destroy and consume: thus it becomes what it fears, and inflicts it on others.

However appalling the prospect, the reality of at least the state of hell (if not the place) has to be faced, because it is true. We can see the evidence of it in living beings in our own neighbourhoods if we dare to look (although mercifully not too frequently). The theological concept of hell is the possibility of this state, that we can see, becoming complete in a person, and therefore final and forever after death. Even then we know that there are no limits to the mercy of God. We do not know for certain of any person who has ever lived who is actually in hell.

There are lesser states of fear, of course, quite distressing enough in their own right. There are people living in constant fear and torment over real or imagined disasters. They live in worlds of their own because hell is always private hell. They cannot relate, cannot love, cannot be happy. They can sometimes, thank God, be helped.

We all have our own ways of thinking about the appearance of hell. The mediaevals furnished it with burning oil and thumbscrews. The New Testament has a lake of fire and brimstone. I sometimes imagine it as full of hot, crowded, noisy basements with lurid lights and violence; or as dead silence: grey, rubbishy, desolate, abandoned; utterly boring. Others see it as closed in or dark. Darkness is another biblical image, of course; but darkness can also be rich and alive and stirring. I love the dark!

Christianity is about the triumph of love and peace over fear and hate. How is this brought about?

A psychologist friend used to say, "The facts are friendly!" There is nothing like a few healthy facts to counter imagined fears. And the fact is that Christ is stronger than hell. We can never, never drop below his mercy and his hands. He can save, and will save, if we call on him.

Sometimes the only way out of our own hells on this earth is through the help of another person. If someone shares the problem with you, you are no longer alone, which is already a relief. Love overcomes fear, and if a person in fear can learn to love unselfishly, without thought of return, this can be their way out of hell. To do this, there needs to be an object for their love — preferably a person. Part of our ministry can sometimes be to allow the unloved and unlovable to love us. If there is no one to whom they relate, how can they focus outgoing love?

Lesser fears are often connected with the fear of loss: loss of a loved one, loss of esteem, loss of possessions. If a person can be brought to the point of freely giving that which they are afraid to lose, at least in thought, that is the deepest antidote to fear. Submission of all into the sure hands of the Lord can be a way of doing this, but the more specific one can be, the deeper the healing.

Sin always creates a blockage in our ability to love, therefore always creates a further area in which fear can operate. The culpable refusal to love, to trust, to live, opens the door to a depth of fear horrible to contemplate, because ultimately it is a complete "No" to God and all that he is. It does incalculable damage to our humanity because we were made to love and to grow in love and understanding. But it is where we would all be without the saving grace of Christ, because one act leads to another and without his help we would get deeper and deeper into sin and despair. Hell refers to the ultimate and complete state of evil, as heaven refers to complete and final bliss. We do not necessarily have to believe anyone reaches this final state, but the evidence for the existence of every other state in between is before our eyes.

Tradition holds that it was the sight of people blundering into hell that caused Jesus' extreme anguish in Gethsemane, and strengthened his resolve to go through the Passion. Because he also has been through the anguish of pain, of terror, of abandonment, of feeling the guilt and the consequence of sin, he can enter the experience of anyone, at whatever depth, and relate to them and bring them through.

13. Abandonment

One of the most anguished cries through the ages is the cry, "I have been left alone!" It is the core of all grief, the heart of abandonment, the sinew of rejection. We have been abandoned in the fight, left alone when we needed help. You could have helped, but you were not there. I had to manage alone! All the struggle was borne alone; and no one now knows me and what I bore.

A common example of this is that of a parent who, for one reason or another, has been left alone to shoulder the responsibility of bringing up the family. It is part of the pain of a bereavement: there is no one now to share in decisions. So one of the most helpful forms of recreation is to be taken out by someone who makes all the decisions!

This feeling of abandonment can turn into a deep fury and resentment at the person or circumstances which caused the situation.

However well we actually coped with the situation at the time, a sense of injustice remains with us. It seems to me that we are left with two needs: a need to share that sense with the person concerned, if there is one such identifiable person; and a need to bring it to a Father, or person with authority, who will somehow 'take' it, accept it, and eventually take on the issues of justice. More than anything, we need to share it with someone who will console us by meeting us and knowing us in the extremity in which we have found ourselves having to cope.

However well we coped with the extraordinary circumstances at the time, there has been a violation to the human self, an injustice to our feelings, which needs to be rectified. With health, with the restoration of the 'normal', there comes a sense of outrage. This needs to be expressed. Life itself has been threatened, at depth. As a baby roars at injury or deprivation, we need to roar in outrage! When we express frustration and anger at the prison walls, we are in fact making an affirmation of ultimate justice, of life, of right values: "This is not right!" In proclaiming our passions and our soul, in vehement terms, we condemn death, destruction, false values, injustice. If this is not expressed, how can we continue to think truly?

We have become so sophisticated in the restraint of our feelings, that we have almost denied their truth. However, the modem ministry of counselling and listening goes a long way to redressing the imbalance into which we have fallen.

We are never meant to be alone permanently, even though solitude may be an important part of our life. We need to tell our stories, like the heroes of old. We need to tell them to our peers. We belong in communities, in spite of our desire sometimes to get away from everyone and to be alone; and for the 'human' side of our personalities to be fulfilled, we need to express ourselves in community. This does not mean sharing our soul-experience with all comers! But our social relationships also have eternal validity, and we cannot ultimately ignore this. Sooner or later our actions and desires have to bear the scrutiny of others. We do not have the right to 'contract out' of being human, nor to say that we are accountable to God alone. We are part of humanity, and our actions and motivations are part of the whole.

Perhaps we underestimate the divine/human nature of Jesus. We also, if we are baptised into him, grow in two natures, the divine and the human. Our difficulties come when they are not integrated as they were in him.

So we need also to tell our woes to an authority figure. We need to experience the deep wisdom that understands and consoles, and which also says, "Well done". We need that deep assurance that we have done well; that it is all right; that it is over now and that we are safe. Without that, we can become demoralised; completely discouraged, with no heart to go on.

Without outside judgment, we can only be the judge of our own actions. Part of us has to adjudicate on the conflict, or it remains unresolved in our minds. But if we adjudicate for ourselves, who adjudicates on that bit of us? The adjudicator in us remains alone — and, like the rest of our complex personalities, cries out in pain for union.

We need and want to be judged. Judgment is what we want in order for the world to settle into place and become secure, taken for granted, so that we may relax and live and play and be creative. Yet, if we rely too much on such judgment, we can remain children, afraid to take risks, and afraid to live in a world that is not in fact safe. Once again a threefold pattern emerges. First, we are children with safe rules. Then we grow and suffer in a world of insecurity and development. Finally, we rest back in the Certain. Perhaps there is continual dynamic movement between these three levels once we have explored each of them: a constant rhythm and movement, like the seasons, where all is changed yet the basic pattern remains. Winter reflects the still, unchanging, basic landscapes; spring is the season of life, development, movement; summer, the fullness of growth; autumn, fruitfulness and dying. Stability and movement are constant motifs of life, and so of God.

There is no rest without judgment. We are restless until we hear the judgment, and receive it. As St. Augustine says that our hearts are restless until they find their rest in God, so judgment is also of the heart — and the judgment of God is merciful and kind.

Judgment also helps our mind to think truly again. Our mind is surely formed by our actions. Once we have done something, that fact creates a feeling of rightness just by being done. If you do a wrong thing once, it is always easier to do it again. Judgment rectifies this.

But to avoid discouragement, we need our good acts to be judged as well. With no appreciation, the worm turns. We say, "I have coped, and I have acted and I have given, and can go no further until I am seen and heard and loved."

We can get to the point when the abandonment has gone on too long, and we no longer care for the appreciation. It was not there when we needed it and were crying out for it, so what does it mean now? It is too late. The relationship has been broken and the appreciation now has no meaning. I think many, many people feel like that today. They cannot be consoled, because there is no relationship within which it can come. Affirmation has to be in the context of a relationship — otherwise we say,

"What right have they to judge my actions? They are nothing to me!" The abandoned one has to be wooed back into a relationship first, before the deeper healing can be made possible.

To preach judgment without a relationship is a nonsense, and to practise it, extraordinarily damaging, whether it be by relatives, teachers or priests; but judgment from within a good relationship is deeply healing, and deeply consoling. And just, loving judgment on oneself and one's relationships can bring the resolution of rage.

So who, in today's world, judges? We have lost faith in authority. We are a fatherless generation. (That is probably why authoritarian sects flourish.)

Right judgment leads directly to praise. Right judgment restores the relationship within which praise can operate.

If we relate the experience to spirituality, then we can say that we are sharing the loneliness of Jesus, which was shown in its extreme in the Agony in Gethsemane, where he fought the duels of fear alone. On the cross we are faced with his agonised cry of dereliction. He felt abandonment by the Father; he also knew that his close friends had gone away. Mary and John were there, with some others — but even then, he was high up, physically away from them. And even in the extremity of that pain, he was hassled: by passers-by, and by those on the neighbouring crosses. Yet it was through those very hassles that some comfort was brought: the thief expressed faith in Jesus, and Jesus was able to give to him — an assurance that that day he would be with him in Paradise. What meaning does this give to our experiences? That when we are totally 'down', and still we are hassled, even in that situation we may bring some good out of it. And we are in a real sense sharing his experience on the cross. Somehow, these cruel experiences have their part in the story of redemption. Martha and Mary, when Lazarus was dying, had the cruel wait to endure, knowing all the time that if Jesus were there, Lazarus would not die; but Jesus delayed, and did not come, and Lazarus did die. Jesus was their special friend. For them of all people, surely he would come. But Lazarus died and was buried. Yes, when Jesus did come he was brought to life again, and the explanation given was that it was so that God's glory could be shown. But the sense of betrayal, of being let down, of being abandoned, was real, and was hard, and remained until it was taken up into this fuller, deeper truth and reason. At the human level it remained an offence.

These fuller levels of meaning come from 'below' the passion level, sweeping the hurts we have suffered up and out of us. The memories may remain, but hopefully the bitterness is gone. Truly, our humanity has to die, before we are resurrected. We fight our own death, but resurrection comes through submission and passivity; and waiting to be raised. Rightly we pray, "Pray for us sinners now, and at the hour of our death"; perhaps we should say, "and at the hours of our many deaths".

There is nevertheless a time for these deaths. We have no right to remain passive in the face of injustice or evil, which should rightly be fought and countered. Jesus many times confronted evil and banished it. We should pray for the discernment to know when we should resist, and when the time has come, or the situation has arisen, where we should remain passive in the face of the inevitable.

"Going the second mile" relates to a situation where "your enemy has forced you to go a mile with him". In going the second mile, we absorb the force of will, and drown it in our free decision to go further, thus somehow neutralising it. So sometimes we may feel it right to let the evil do its worst, and assess the damage at the end. If the force is irresistible, we must bow beneath it (but without compromise); even though it does sometimes mean we are lifted out by the roots.

The attacker sometimes loses interest and decides he does not want what he has gained; eventually withdraws. Or the episode leads to a new situation which is acceptable. History bears witness to the eventual resolution of particular conflicts.

This leads back directly to the twofold dynamic of spiritual life: active and passive. There is a place for active resistance and action and growth of new things; and a place for passive resistance, suffering, and the neutralising of evil. The neutralising of evil prepares the soil in which the new growth can take root and flourish. Sacrifice and death are the necessary prelude to resurrection.

14. Winning the Battle: Resurrection

At last we reach the Resurrection! Resurrection joy is real and does not happen just at Easter. After taking such a good, hard look at evil and suffering, it is very easy to get discouraged. In fact, to look round at the difficulties of the world is a sure route to depression! I think that is why listening to the news is often too much for people. We hear of all the 'downs', but very few of the 'ups'. I was once told that we should never think of the Passion and Crucifixion without also thinking of the Resurrection. Suffering is not the last word!

Christian life is a battle, a struggle — but we were never promised a rose-garden. "In the world you will have trouble, but be of good cheer — I have overcome the world" (John 16:33). Resurrection signifies victory in the battle: it never meant that there would be no battle. The Resurrection Lord is a Lord of vigour, of laughter, of strength, but the battle was won in apparent weakness.

Moments of resurrection joy are certainly experienced in this life on many occasions. We do not have to wait until we die!

I am a great lover of fantasy literature. Much of this starts with a call: a call to the hero (who as yet does not know he is a hero). He is told more about the world he lives in: he sees the forces of good and evil at play. He is shown by the 'wizard' or 'wise' figure the true state of affairs (too frightening for ordinary folk to know about), and is asked whether he will respond to the call.

From then on, because he says 'yes', his life is transformed. One danger and difficulty follows another, but somehow, though at cost, he always wins through.

Very often he conquers a dragon. If the dragon is killed, his treasures are made available to the hero. If he is tamed, his reformed personality adds a new dimension of help to the hero's life.

Apart from the hero and the ordinary folk, there is usually a third range of people: those in authority, those with armies and skills, who fight the threatened evil in a deliberate but more 'normal' way.

After the battles, when things return to a new and peaceful stage, there is often a feeling of anti-climax. Peace seems extremely difficult to write about. The next volume in the saga usually starts with fresh difficulties, a fresh challenge and a new fight.

Some people in life are called to see more; they see the same facts as others, but they are caught by their significance and challenged to respond. One way of helping a person to find their sphere of service is to ask who they care about; what stories in the news engage their real attention; where do they feel the most compassion.

The individual who responds may either be part of the main forces, engaging in day-to-day battle with an acknowledged evil or threat; or occasionally they are in fact the hero figure: the one who somehow is alone, who bears the brunt, carries the main burden. He or she may be fighting a lone battle some distance from the main scene of battle; may even be someone terminally ill or caring for someone who is. But the heroic is a component of all good causes.

Heroic love does not need to be dramatic; much more often it lies in the mundane. It lies in the refusal to be bitter; the option to stay loving; the acceptance and setting aside of disappointment, or even of grief, after due time. It is difficult to opt for happiness, and all the responsibilities that it brings. It is difficult, but ungenerous love is ugly. We have all seen it. To love without thought of return is liberating and brings joy, but it can also bring a human backlash. If we have really put ourselves out and given generously of our time and our energy, when the event is over and we feel tired and a bit 'flat', we can resent all those who did not work as hard as we did. It is very common, but it spoils things. Above all, it spoils our own joy in giving. The complaints are always justified! But if we are not careful, we are the losers twice over. When we repent and are forgiven, then our joy is increased.

The permanent experience of joy is not ours any more than it was Jesus'. Nor should it be. Nothing isolates us more from non-Christians than a failure to have shared in their experiences of loneliness, cold, grief, anxiety, emptiness, meaninglessness. It is only through experiencing these things, and somehow finding Christ in them (and hence, meaning), that we can begin to help others.

Jesus experienced real depth anguish in Gethsemane and throughout his passion. So was he joyful? Surely in the depths of his being he knew that he was doing the Father's will. Because of that, at any instant, joy, in a form we would recognise, could shoot through what was happening (as, for instance, when he was able to assure the thief on the next cross that he would shortly be with him in Paradise). I suggest he had a latent joy. And it is that latent joy that we can aim for. We cannot guarantee how often it will envelop our whole consciousness, but in the middle of sorrow, difficulty, anxiety, we can be aware of a latent joy because we are ultimately, at depth, trying with all our heart and strength to do the will of the Father, in him. And this is the source of our joy.

This joy is a gift, but a gift we can ask for. It is one of the fruits of the Spirit, and the Spirit is a gift to the church and all those who constitute it. Like all gifts of the Spirit, our task is to prepare ourselves, in Christ, to receive it.

I would love to be able to say to someone, "Trust in God, and all will be all right," as some Christians seem to say. But I don't think that that is true. Ultimately, yes, he will be with us, even if we do not feel him, in all the difficulties, and in the worst of them. When the world was set in motion, I believe that Jesus committed himself to coming to share in it, and in all the worst of its mistakes, before he even knew what they would be. How else could he justify the way in which it was created, and the risks built into it?

We are all led along different paths, and all the evidence points to the fact that some are asked to bear more than others. It depends on whether you are called to be a hero, or a fighter, or one of the ordinary folk. But even the ordinary folk are called to play very important parts. They are the backdrop against which the dramas are played; the fabric on which the design is worked. It is immensely important that they play their parts as ordinary folk; they will find their own dramas in the playing.

Life seems to be strung on two poles: the large and the small. Look large, and against the stars and the galaxies you see the hero figures, like the Norse gods of ancient days; or the great saints of the church. Look small, and you see the same configurations and wonders and miracles in the smallest atom or situation. There is no situation too small to contain a hero.

It doesn't really matter which battle we are fighting (so long as the cause is honourable): the important thing is to keep believing in victory. And if visible victory is not granted to us, then our efforts can be turned into a sacrifice and be made fruitful in another way. Ultimately, victory is assured. All our real victories are kept very safe for us in heaven, even if we feel we are immediately thrown right back into the fray after only a brief respite. All heaven is around us; a dimension of all that we do. We are surrounded with the "great crowd of witnesses" who are perhaps even envious, if that is possible, that we are still able to work and suffer for the Lord; still able to accrue yet more victories for his Name.

Somehow the hero in fiction does win through, even if he loses his or her life in the process. After long and bitter struggles, the final disaster is averted. We would not accept it otherwise. We would look for the sequel when the meaning of the events would be made plain to us, and we would see that in fact it had all turned out for the best. Such is our nature. In the depths of the human heart, there is a final, unquenchable hope that all will be well. Surely such hope is true.

What about rest or respite — holidays? Most sagas have episodes where friends meet and there is a temporary let-up in the fight or struggle. The interesting thing is that, although most of the action is concerned with the fighting, the periods of respite do in fact feel to be the 'norm', from which fighting is a distraction.

In life, to hope and continue to hope and believe that peace and harmony are the 'norm' is often very difficult. But when we do the opposite and accept the difficulties, the problems and the worries as the 'norm', even if they are the main component of our lives, then we open the doors to cynicism, depression and even despair.

It may be normal to have difficulties, and unrealistic to think otherwise, but just as with a book or a film when the greater part is about difficulties but the theme is the overcoming of them, so the true life, that for which we are made, is surely that which we only enjoy from time to time: peace, harmony, good and growing relationships, laughter and good fellowship.

There will always be challenges, but they do not have to spring from resisting evil. They can be challenges of achievement in sport or education; of discovery; of art and culture. There will always be 'greats' to aim for. So much of our creative energy is used up in aggression: if only we could divert it back into its proper channels!

What about the end of the story — the 'happy-ever-after' chapters? We cannot envisage them. Human happy-ever-after ideas nearly always come out as boring. Perhaps that is because humanity in its earthly form is not meant to be eternal. Eternity is for transformed, resurrected humanity. The joys will be of a dimension appropriate to this, just as human happiness is appropriate to ordinary humanity. To invest human happiness with selected aspects of post-human joy is bound to sound odd. The whole reality is different.

Sometimes it does help to think of just something that we may expect, so, as a final thought, I offer for reflection these suggestions of what may constitute some of the joys of heaven:
- the joy of engaging in true worship
- the joy of seeing goodness triumph;
- the joy of seeing the intricacy and beauty of God's meaning and of his plans;
- the joy of seeing that all things have worked together for good;
- the joy of the love, the beauty, and the wisdom of the Trinity;
- the joy of seeing how we have been allowed to participate in the plan for redeeming the world, by our work and our prayers, our suffering and our joy;

- the joy of seeing how we have been allowed to serve Jesus, and been used by him;
- the joy of seeing how others have been beautified by him and have served him;
- the joy of seeing how the events that most distressed us became the source of our deepest enrichment, and how our efforts — so hard at the time — have in fact borne fruit in glory.

Let us live in hope and joy and love, in the certain hope of knowing that we shall at last, with relatives and friends, be at peace and be able to praise, worship, love, laugh and even be creative because we shall be living in the God who sustains all life.

The rest is mystery.